Anita Mai Genua | Clare Davenport
Elizabeth Lenell Davies

111 Places in Toronto That You Must Not Miss

Photographs by Clare Davenport

emons:

We would like to dedicate this book lovingly to our
spirited mothers, who encouraged us to embrace adventure.
Their call to courage pushed us to explore both near and far.
Thank you Helgi, Sheila, and Barbara.

MIX
Papier aus verantwor-
tungsvollen Quellen
FSC® C083411

© Emons Verlag GmbH
All rights reserved
© Photographs: Clare Davenport, except: see p. 237
© Cover motif: shutterstock.com/vichie81
Layout: Eva Kraskes, based on a design
by Lübbeke | Naumann | Thoben
Edited by Karen E. Seiger
Maps: altancicek.design, www.altancicek.de
Basic cartographical information from Openstreetmap,
© OpenStreetMap-Mitwirkende, ODbL
Printing and binding: CPI – Clausen & Bosse, Leck
Printed in Germany 2018
ISBN 978-3-7408-0257-8
First edition

Did you enjoy it? Do you want more?
Join us in uncovering new places around the world on:
www.111places.com

Foreword

The evolution of *111 Places in Toronto That You Must Not Miss* has been a journey of discovery into the farthest corners and hidden spaces in this exemplary, multi-seasoned metropolis. Originally created by the blending of Indigenous and British cultures, the city has moved to the forefront of the world's imagination, helping to define a new global culture.

This book has provided us with a playful reason to explore "Muddy York," as Toronto was known in its early days, with a vengeance. Despite having lived in the 6ix, so nicknamed for its six boroughs, our entire adult lives, we discovered countless layers, both traditional and edgy, to this quickly transforming city. Its urban spirit became our treasure trove, and its varied landscape our map. Along the way, we met with an astounding and inspiring assortment of artists, adventurers, business owners, and curators.

We invite you, residents and visitors alike, to come with us and hike our beautiful inner city trails along the many ravines, no matter the season. Paddle a canoe to Indigenous bridges, or don a toque and come tobogganing and skating with the locals. Take the longest streetcar ride in North America through flourishing neighbourhoods that will reveal their hidden gems to you. Find small artisanal ice creameries and sake breweries in crumbling limestone buildings. Wander the graffiti alleys, or listen to world-class musicians at a goth-baroque cocktail lounge. And if there is still time, consider finishing your day by uncovering a mystery in a Canadian Castle and dining in a Vietnamese tapas hideaway.

This guidebook is a love letter, a way for us to share with you our appreciation for Toronto. We are thankful to our city for providing a progressive and safe urban environment where we can play, grow, work and nurture families in the place we call home.

Please come experience the allure of the 6ix for yourselves!

With love, Anita, Clare, and Elizabeth

111 Places

1 Adonis Middle Eastern Grocer

Come be mesmerized by puffed-up pita pillows

Heading east on Eglinton along Toronto's Golden Mile, one of Canada's first industrial areas, you will find a massive, red-trimmed glass building. It is easily mistakable for a gaudy new gym, but do not be deterred. Inside is one of Toronto's most entertaining multicultural grocery experiences.

Adonis is a hybrid of a Middle Eastern *souk* and a North American megastore. It was founded in 1979, by two Lebanese brothers who escaped to Canada along with a new immigrant's determination to succeed. Entering the sensory showroom, you are greeted by a vast produce section, larger and more bountiful than even the most opulent of grocery chains. Interestingly, the fruit and vegetable displays, many of which are unrecognizable, occupy the entire front section of the store. Behind is a maze of aisles against a large, glass backdrop enclosing a piece of shiny stainless machinery. This large glasshouse, surrounded by curious onlookers, is home to the famous Adonis pita-making machine. With the pita being a mainstay of the Middle Eastern diet, it is logical that this important food element is at the forefront of this remarkable experience. As the machine pumps out 6,000 pita pockets a day, you can become mesmerized watching the dough expand into puffed-up pillows.

Don't stay hypnotized – visit the outer displays. Indulge in a large assortment of olives or nuts. Sample an exotic, freshly squeezed juice. The halloumi and feta cheese display stretches on for miles. The meat counter is full of fresh cuts, pre-marinated meats and an array of animal parts. Stop by the prepared section for a well-priced samosa, kebab, shawarma or falafel. If there is still room, conclude your visit at the endlessly caloric baklava bar. With gracious staff willing to provide samples, you will be wearing a honey-sweetened smile in no time.

Address 20 Ashtonbee Road, Scarborough, ON M1L 3K9, +1 (416)642-1515, www.groupeadonis.ca/en/ontario | Getting there By car, drive along Eglinton Avenue (east of Victoria Park Avenue), then turn north on Hakimi Avenue to Ashtonbee Road | Hours Mon–Sat 9am–10pm, Sun 9am–9pm | Tip If you would like to complete your ethnic experience, stop by Vienna Fine Foods on Birchmount. It is an exquisite Austrian and German deli. Complete with European canned and bottled gourmet goods, potato salads, cold cuts and schnitzel, it will satisfy the guests at your next gathering (1050 Birchmount Road, Scarborough, ON M1K 1S4, www.viennafinefoods.com).

2 Aga Khan Park

A 21st-century Islamic masterpiece

Perched elegantly above the Don Valley in a neighbourhood of low rises, is The Aga Khan Park. This majestic, 17-acre green space is gracefully bookended between two Islamic gems: the Aga Khan Museum and the Ismaili Centre. The garden gives visitors a space to reflect, a welcome counterbalance to the intricate and ornate Islamic art exhibits inside.

Beirut landscape architect Vladimir Djurovic designed this urban sanctuary. An advisor to the Aga Khan came across Djurovic's work purely by chance, as he comes from a relatively small architectural firm. The architect was encouraged by the Aga Khan to visit traditional gardens worldwide. The result is a 21st-century masterpiece: a garden which is as much about stimulating your non-visual senses as your visual ones.

Entering the park, you are struck by the natural geometry of the five large reflecting pools in a field of soft gravel. It is a modern take on a traditional four-part garden and a powerful Islamic metaphor for the organization and domestication of the landscape. Unlike English gardens, which are designed for walking, Islamic gardens are intended for restful contemplation. Do sit and take it all in. The black pools offset the purple Russian sage and orderly planting of serviceberry trees. The methodical serenity is breathtaking. Visitors tend to be quiet—meditative perhaps. Local office workers lunch while families frolic. The soothing water sounds cancel the nearby traffic. The gardens flow outside of the cedar-hedged perimeter. Spot the birds and butterflies, thoughtfully attracted to the plantings. Pay attention to the wide assortment of trees, carefully selected for their varying shapes and brawny ability to withstand winters.

Though eight miles out of the city core, this green jewel is not to be missed. Come explore this botanical testament to Toronto's multicultural spirit.

Address 77 Wynford Drive, North York, ON M3C 1K1, +1 (416)646-4677, www.agakhanpark.org | **Getting there** Subway to Eglinton (Line 1), then take 34C Eglinton East bus to Wynford Drive; by car (southbound), take the Don Valley Parkway (DVP) to Wynford Drive and turn right; or (northbound), take the Don Valley Parkway, exit Eglinton Avenue westbound, turn right on Don Mills Road, and right on Wynford Drive | **Hours** Daily 6am–10pm | **Tip** The elegant Diwan Restaurant at the adjacent Aga Khan Museum boasts global fare inspired by the Middle East, Turkey, and India. Make sure to reserve ahead (77 Wynford Drive, North York, ON M3C 1K1, www.agakhanmuseum.org).

3__Al Purdy Statue

Dead poet with a Twitter account

Sitting on the side of a stately, old-growth park, which surrounds an equally stately Queen's Park Legislative Building, is an irreverent statue of Al Purdy, dead poet.

His gangly frame is draped upon a rock, and he's resting a book on his leg as he gazes at Queen's Park, Ontario's governmental centre. Did he know when he was alive that there would be a Twitter account (@statuteofalpurdy) created for his statue? If you read the last stanza in his poem, 'The Dead Poet', "expect just a small whisper / of the birds nesting and green things growing / and a brief saying of them / and know where the words come from," maybe the people's poet extraordinaire had a small inkling that this might be the case.

Al Purdy was a big, lanky man, whom broadcaster Pamela Wallen described as 'a cross between Shakespeare and a vaudeville comedian.' With a rough and tumble honesty thick with drinking, imagery and raw description, Al Purdy was a poet for the Everyman who genuinely loved his home province. In Toronto, we only had the statue of Scottish poet Robbie Burns erected in 1902. This changed when the who's who of the Canadian literati set came together and arrived at a decision that a statue of Al Purdy had to be erected facing the Ontario legislature. As sculptor Dam de Nogales observed, 'It's our politicians we honour, but the voice of the people and the voice of the land is often more beautifully and genuinely expressed by the voice of the poets.'

Charles Bukowski once said, 'I don't know of any good living poets. But there's this tough son of a bitch up in Canada that walks the line.' One of the best and most celebrated documentaries at Toronto International Film Festival 2015 was, *Al Purdy was Here*, which explained how Purdy inspired a whole generation of Canadian songwriters. Go and see the bronze statue of Purdy, and tweet out an ode to him.

Address Queen's Park, 110 Wellesley Street West, Toronto, ON M7A | Getting there
Subway to Queen's Park (Line 1); 506 Carlton streetcar to College Street and University
Avenue; subway to Museum (Line 1) | Hours Unrestricted | Tip Just north of the statue,
the Royal Ontario Museum, Canada's largest museum, features a 2007 extension known as
the 'Crystal', designed by Michael Lee-Chin. It is a striking, angular building that was quite
controversial for its deconstructivist design (100 Queen's Park, Toronto, ON M5S 2C6,
www.rom.on.ca/en).

4 Alexander Wood Statue
The Inspector General of private accounts

During the sexual revolution of the 1960s, Canada, as a nation, was at the forefront of the decriminalization of homosexuality. Our prime minister at the time, Pierre Elliott Trudeau, proclaimed, 'The state has no business in the bedrooms of the nation.' Things were very different in the early 1800s for Alexander Wood, a Scottish merchant and magistrate in Upper Canada. This is a story of how a scandalous reputation transformed into heroic adulation.

Wood found himself inadvertently playing the lead role in a sex scandal when investigating a rape case in 1810. The victim, a Miss Bailey, claimed that she did not know the assailant's identity; however, she had scratched his penis. Aha, a clue! Wood personally inspected the genitals of many youthful suspects. There is no evidence that Wood acted improperly during the investigation, but contradictory rumours began to spread about his conduct. Was there really a Miss Bailey after all, or was this a ruse to seduce young men? This was a serious allegation at the time, since sodomy was punishable by death. Wood was nicknamed, 'The Inspector General of Private Accounts' by York society, and also called 'Molly,' a derogatory slang term for a homosexual.

In 1827, Wood purchased 50 acres of land mockingly called 'Molly Wood's Bush'. It is now the location of Toronto's gay village. The area presently pays homage to the man, with street names such as Alexander Street, Wood Street and an Alexander Place. Alas, no Molly street exists.

The Church Wellesley Village Business Association, in 2005, commissioned the artist Dee Newbigging to create a life-size bronze sculpture of Alexander Wood, immortalizing him as the forefather of Toronto's gay community. As opposed to emoting shame, Wood's effigy proudly sports a rose on his lapel, the same rose Pierre Elliott Trudeau consistently wore and changed our laws and attitudes forever.

Address Corner of Church Street and Alexander Street, Toronto, ON M4Y 2C7 |
Getting there Subway to College (Line 1) | Hours Unrestricted | Tip Buddies in Bad
Times Theatre is an alternative theatre and showcases 'artistically rigorous' productions
that often promote LGBT voices (12 Alexander Street, Toronto, ON M4Y 1B4,
www.buddiesinbadtimes.com).

5 Allan Gardens Conservatory

Take a holiday in an urban botanical oasis

Down the street from the formerly gritty 'Hooker Harvey's', lies the grand old dame of historic greenhouse finery. It does not bear the modern, antiseptic urban aesthetic, rather it is a nod to the grace of a former era. Whether you like succulents or the stunning eye pop of multicoloured blooms during the famous Spring and Easter Flower Show, you will be delighted at every turn in this 16,000-square-foot botanical wonderland. It's oxygenated urban therapy for your lungs and mind.

Situated on a five-acre plot of land generously donated by George William Allan, the 11th mayor of Toronto, Allan Gardens, along with Queen's Park, formed the beginning of horticulture and park systems in Toronto. The conservatory was once home to a great pavilion which, at its time in the late 1800s, was Toronto's cultural centre. Even the likes of Oscar Wilde would come and give lectures in this grand building. As Toronto's oldest park, it is a home to a bountiful bouquet of Torontonians too. Its free admission invites everyone from the homeless to the super rich, a student artist, to a family of new Canadians enjoying the tropical orchids and the turtles by the water wheel.

Wandering through the six climatic glass enclosures, Canadians suffering the winter blues will get a chlorophyll blast and flowerpower teleportation away from ornery Old Man Winter, and also the oppressive humidity of August. With over 30 movie shoots a year, the conservatory attracts movie stars and romantics alike. From nervous first dates to heartfelt engagements, the flora awakens a part in ourselves that can be hard to find in our frantic urban lifestyles.

And as plants renew themselves, so will Allan Gardens. The city is planning for a transformation, which will feature new gardens, art exhibits, and a cafe. Visit Toronto's historic garden oasis as it enters a new age of popularity.

Address 19 Horticultural Avenue, Toronto, ON M5A 2P2, +1 (416)392-7288, www.toronto.ca | Getting there 506 Carlton streetcar to Jarvis Street; 141 Downtown/ Mount Pleasant Express bus to Jarvis Street at Carlton Street | Hours Daily 10am–5pm | Tip For a beautiful, Victorian-inspired, exterior garden experience, visit St. James Park by St. James Cathedral (120 King Street East, Toronto, ON M5C 1G6, www.toronto.ca).

6 Arctic Bites

Ice grilling with milk and cream

Who could imagine that four great friends would cement their friendship around -20°C cooling plates? In 2016, Arctic Bites, inspired by the street vendors of Thailand, opened in the eclectic Baldwin Village neighbourhood and restaurant row. As a newcomer to the artisanal ice cream scene, it rises above the rest because of its magical method of production and its creatively refreshing flavours.

Come and enter the popular ice cream factory, home of the mascot 'Poppy the Penguin'. Join the line-up and peer through the glass, as you patiently enjoy the visual experience of the hand-crafted ice cream rolls being created. Although known throughout Thailand as 'stir-fried ice cream', these methods are relatively undiscovered in Canada. As a pancake-like batter is poured onto the ice grill, the concoction is vigorously hand mixed and chopped as it slowly freezes. Toppings are mixed in with focus and patience. The ice cream freezes into thin layers, which are carefully cut and rolled into the crafted polar-rolls. It is pure ice cream artistry. The ice cream making process begins with only milk and cream, omitting the additives, preservatives, stabilizers, and emulsifiers that you will see in most other ice creams. As Arctic Bites flash freeze their carefully tailored dairy concoction on the spot, their end product becomes more flavourful and much creamier than store bought ice creams.

Although the flavours change often, you can always rely on some standard favourites. We're Mint To Be includes not only Oreo cookie crumbs but also Mint Oreo ice cream and a dab of whipped cream with a chocolate drizzle. It Takes Two To Mango, complete with mango ice cream, lychee jelly and diced mango, makes your tongue tingle. Although the entire production process takes two to three minutes per serving, this boutique ice cream store will reward your pallet and your patience.

Address 21 Baldwin Street, Toronto, ON M5T 1L1, +1 (647)347-2818, www.arcticbites.com |
Getting there 510 Spadina streetcar to Nassau Street and head south to Baldwin Street;
506 Carlton streetcar to McCaul Street and head south to Baldwin Street; 505 Dundas
streetcar to McCaul Street and continue north to Baldwin Street | Hours Sun–Thu 1–9pm,
Fri & Sat 1–10pm | Tip The entire Baldwin area is full of great restaurants. If you feel
like an unpretentious bistro with a garden patio, serving inventive French fare, try Bodega
(30 Baldwin Street, Toronto, ON M5T 1L3, www.bodegarestaurant.com).

7 Assembly Chef's Hall

Google me gourmet food truck hipster hall

On the first floor of Google's headquarters in Toronto, a new phenomenon has been unleashed, one which seems to be taking over big cities in North America: the chef-driven community market. If you wish to taste some of the most current inventions of 17 celebrated chefs under one roof, Chef's Assembly Hall is the answer to your culinary desires. Most of the chefs have a satellite restaurant or catering business from which they pivot, but all are attracted to the 500,000 potential foodies who use the PATH network in Toronto's financial district and have easy access to the location at Richmond and York.

Delicious food is not the only sensory experience assembled in this 18,000-square-foot adult culinary playground. As you enter, you will see the DJ as he nods his head to the techno beat, and an old Western movie playing in the background. Lights, neon signage, separate cocktail and wine bars, and cavernous seating arrangements make this venue feel like a 21st-century urban Valhalla.

Toronto has its share of restaurants offering various food stations, such as the Marché Movenpick. In comparison, the Chef's Assembly Hall offers a food-truck vibe, with the emphasis being on new twists of multicultural fare offered up casually. What makes it so special is that after you have ordered your food, you are able to sit down to a full modern dining experience. It's a far cry from sitting on an aging picnic table in the middle of a parking lot, which is often the case with food trucks.

Lobster bisque from Nova Scotia, gourmet coffee, Thai street food, southern fried chicken, and imaginative plant protein expressions of all sorts are just some of the delicious offerings that defy you to call this place a food court. Add any style of libation that you can imagine, as you sit down, and you too will start to nod your head along with the DJ as you bite into a chef-inspired delight.

Address 111 Richmond Street West, Toronto, ON M5H 2G4, +1 (647)557-5993,
www.assemblychefshall.com, hello@assemblychefshall.com | Getting there Subway to
Osgoode (Line 1) | Hours Mon–Sat 7am–10pm | Tip Walk east and check out the large
art installation, Flight Stop, by renowned artist John Snow, featuring Canada geese in
flight. The mobile hangs in the southern-most ceiling of Toronto's Eaton Centre
(220 Yonge Street, Toronto, ON M5B 2H1, www.cfshops.com/toronto-eaton-centre.html).

8 Bad Axe Throwing

Release your inner lumberjack

Looking to jazz up your evening, brush up on your hand-eye coordination, or celebrate a vital piece of Canada's history in a completely unique way? Well look no further. Bad Axe Toronto could be your answer to buffing up your inner lumberjack. The throwing of axes has been around since prehistoric times. In terms of Canada, the aboriginals were amazingly skilled with their tomahawks, and the Canadian lumberjacks, born from European New World loggers, cleared swathes of forest by axe alone in the 18th century. As a reprieve from their long hours and dangerous work, the men and their wives (known as lumberjills) entertained themselves in their remote campsites by playing various axe sports.

On the second floor of an office building, you enter an open-concept area set up with six targets that allow three concurrent face-offs to occur. Chain-link fences protect you from any wild throws by neighbours beside you, while tables made from barrels are available for cheering and observing. A place to learn an unlikely skill, socialize, and release pent-up frustration – it's all available under one roof. You are invited to bring your own alcoholic beverages and snacks. The walls are decorated with ominous enemies and villains from history, and the music is loud enough to set off your competitive spirit.

As your turn approaches, and you're feeling particularly uncoordinated, consider it a game of darts – just slightly more dangerous and involving an axe. Perhaps it is your chance to live out that scene from *The Shining* in a nonviolent way. If you feel like your skills are appropriately competitive, you can even join an axe-throwing league. Although league members and staff veterans look like warriors from a J. R. R. Tolkien novel, don't be put off by their hardened veneers. With many types of hatchet and tomahawk options, coupled with excellent professional instruction, the experience will be 'bad axe'.

Address 346 Ryding Avenue, Unit 201, Toronto, ON M6N 1H5, +1 (416)604-4815, www.badaxethrowing.com | Getting there Subway to Runnymede (Line 2), then take the 71 Runnymede North bus to Ryding Avenue | Tip For the adventurous at heart, try the Rock Oasis, fabulous rock climbing facility for people of all ages (388 Carlaw Avenue, Suite 204, Toronto, ON M4M 2T4, www.rockoasis.com).

9 — The Baldwin Steps

Climb the steep slopes of ancient Lake Iroquois

Often the stairs of the past enable us to reach the heights of tomorrow. And so it is with the Baldwin Steps. Hidden at the intersection of Davenport Road and Spadina Avenue, this cascading staircase divides two celebrated Toronto neighbourhoods: the tony Annex and sophisticated Forest Hill. The steps, which date back to the 19th century, are located on the dramatic, 12,000-year-old shore cliff of the ancient Lake Iroquois, a distant relative of Lake Ontario. The shoreline eventually became known today as Davenport Road and, because of its steep nature, hampered and humbled early settlers.

Originally made of wood, the staircase is now a zigzagging collection of cement and concrete risers. The steps are all but hidden by the mature, terraced gardens during the spring and summer seasons. Surprisingly, this public pathway was the location of the proposed Spadina expressway in the 1960s, and since the 1980s, it has been home to the Spadina Subway, which runs deep underground. Although the land was leased by the city of Toronto in 1984, it was once owned by the Baldwin lineage, a well-to-do Toronto family. William Baldwin was a well-respected government official and a designer of the north-south Spadina corridor.

Get your cardio for the day as you puff to the top of the 111 steps along with many athletic Torontonians. Take a moment to pause and pirouette, soaking in the views from the spacious platforms during your climb. Reaching the stairs' summit, discover the grand, unobstructed view of the Spadina Avenue reaching to today's Lake Ontario. Grab a drink from the water fountain and a stop at a nearby bench to take in Toronto. Wonder along the cliff top, perhaps visiting the exquisite Casa Loma to the west and the undiscovered gardens of Spadina House, both celebrating Toronto's wealthiest neighbourhood from the 1900s, and the glorious splendor of a bygone era.

Address 486 Davenport Road, Toronto, ON M5R 1X8, www.tclf.org/landscapes/
Baldwin-steps.com | **Getting there** Subway to Dupont (Line 1) and walk north to
Davenport Road | **Hours** Unrestricted | **Tip** Learn about life in Toronto between
1900 and 1930 at the Spadina House Museum in the Austin family house. Exhibits
include the family's papers, music, art and décor, as well as tours and events
(285 Spadina Road, Toronto, ON M5R 2V5, www.toronto.ca).

10 Banksy's Guard with Dog

Ephemeral street art for the age

One month before Toronto's infamous G20 summit in 2010, the politically charged British street artist Banksy stenciled seven guerrilla artworks, only two of which remain. *Guard with Balloon Dog* was painted on the limestone facade of the former headquarters of the Ontario Provincial Police. The timely image portrays a security guard holding a pink, muzzled, balloon-sculpture dog, mocking the impotence of authority. The decommissioned building was subsequently bought by Toronto real estate developer Jared Menkes and demolished, save for a 3 x 1.5m series of three slabs on which the graffiti artwork originally appeared.

After painstaking restoration, the Banksy piece has been encased in a whopping one-and-a-half tons of glass. Now housed as a part of the PATH, Toronto's 'damn the seasons' series of pedestrian walkways in the business district, *Guard With Balloon Dog* remains, in spirit, a public art installation.

Artist Joseph Chou created a companion piece, a massive, arched stainless-steel reflector called *Speculum*, which reveals the Banksy piece to those who stroll from the development's easternmost entrance, adding a kinetic property to the limestone slabs.

The juxtaposition of such a darkly humorous, anti-authoritarian artwork in the midst of the well-heeled, this critique of capitalism can be justified in part by the Banksy manifesto, 'Any advert in a public space that gives you no choice whether you see it or not is yours. It's yours to take, rearrange and re-use.' Appraised at $875,000, Banksy's act of vandalism has turned out to be a great boon for a commercial development corporation and for the city.

Despite, or due to, his international notoriety, Banksy could ride the wave of his renown, renounce his anonymity, and pad his pocket through commissioned works. Instead, he has chosen to remain a mystery and to challenge the art establishment.

Address 1 York Street, PATH Corridor, Toronto, ON M5J 2L9 | **Getting there** Subway to Union (Line 1), walk 0.5 kilometres / 0.3 miles south to corner of York and Harbor Streets, take escalator down to PATH Corridor; 510 Spadina streetcar from Harbourfront Centre to Queens Quay West and walk 275 metres/0.2 miles east to 1 York Centre, take escalator down to PATH Corridor | **Hours** Unrestricted | **Tip** Another Banksy graffiti art piece, protected in plexiglass, is located at the intersection of Church Street and the Esplanade. This is the only other Banksy piece still visible in Toronto.

11 BAPS Shri Swaminarayan Mandir

Celebration of Indo-Canadian community

Adjacent to Highway 427, in a neighbourhood known more for its industrial boxed buildings and aging water parks, is an 18-acre complex with a massive, sparkling, white temple. Evocative of ancient Indian palaces, you are shocked that something so magnificent could exist within city limits. Toronto's own Swaminarayan Mandir is a testament to Toronto's Indo-Canadian community.

This centre of worship is comprised of a *mandir*, or temple, a *haveli*, or modern-day community centre, and a heritage museum. Built by the Swaminarayan branch of Hinduism, who followed ancient scriptures regarding the temple's construction, no ferrous metals were used, but rather heavy layers of stone.

The temple consists of over 24,000 pieces of glistening marble and stone. 1,800 craftsmen throughout India carefully carved the stones, each representing a connection and contribution. The pieces were then numbered and sent to Canada where, over an 18-month period, a community of 400 volunteers came together to re-jigsaw the temple – symbolizing hours of selfless service.

Entering through the grand teak entrance and removing your shoes, you smile when you discover that they have combined ancient architecture with modern amenities to create a heated floor, a warm luxury for barefoot devotees. The light-filled courtyard is surrounded by teak and rosewood columns, beautifully carved with virtuous Hindu deities.

Climbing the staircase to the mandir, your mood shifts as you become peaceful and present. More than a building of stone and marble, the mandir is a living breathing entity, vibrant with the life of the divine. Deities are installed in breathtaking shrines. You pause. Transcending religious and cultural boundaries, the temple celebrates the best of Toronto's multicultural tapestry.

Address 61 Claireville Drive, Etobicoke, ON M9W 5Z7, +1 (416)798-2277, www.baps.org/
toronto, info@canada.baps.org | **Getting there** Subway to Wilson (Line 1), then board
96 Wilson West bus to 61 Clairville Drive | **Hours** Daily 9am–6:30pm | **Tip** Just across the
street from the Mandir is Shayona Foods, serving delicious hot and cold Indian vegetarian
snacks and sweets (46 Claireville Drive, Etobicoke, ON M9W 5T9, +1 (416)987-5097,
www.shayona.org).

12 Barberian's Steak House

Pop a cork to iconic history

It is often said that truth is stranger than fiction, and so it is with Barberian's Steak House. As the youngest of four from an Armenian refugee family, Harry Barberian found it difficult to assimilate into the staunchly Anglican town of Brantford, Ontario. Harry struggled at school, preferring instead more entrepreneurial pursuits, including working for a tractor company, cooking for a circus sideshow and winning and losing restaurants through gambling. By 1958, the entrepreneurial Armenian had purchased the townhouse and former brothel currently known as Barberian's Steak House. Imagine the surprise of Harry's dour high-school principal when he met Harry and his alluring wife riding in their shiny, new Rolls-Royce a few years later.

Barberian's today is as much dedicated to quality food as it is to Canadian history. It houses Hudson Bay Company artefacts and a collection of works by Canada's iconic landscape artists, the Group of Seven. All of Canada's prime ministers have eaten here, as have countless celebrities, including rock stars Mick Jagger and Geddy Lee. Elizabeth Taylor and Richard Burton first got engaged here. Entering the elegant wood-clad restaurant, you are warmly greeted into a cavern of culinary treats and treasures.

Aaron, Harry's son, is as much a character as his father and has taken over the family business since his father's passing. Driven to contribute to his community, he donates millions to charitable causes, honouring Harry's legacy. After a delicious meal of Toronto's best rib eye and classic baked potato with just enough butter and sour cream to delight your taste buds, make sure to visit Aaron's subterranean wine vault. This three-story cellar is the largest in Canada, with close to 20,000 bottles of legendary wines. With artistic beams, hydraulic lifts and gilded chandeliers, it completes this historic steak house.

Address 7 Elm Street, Toronto, ON M5G 1H1, +1 (416)597-0335, www.barberians.com |
Getting there Subway to Dundas (Line 1), then a 300 metre/0.2 mile walk; paid parking lots
and metered street parking | Hours Mon–Fri noon–2:30pm & 5pm–midnight, Sat & Sun
4:30pm–midnight | Tip For a nice stroll after a fabulous meal, consider wandering just south
of Barberian's where you can visit a larger-than-life-sized statue of Sir Winston Churchill in the
northwest corner of Nathan Phillips Square (100 Queen Street West, Toronto, ON M5H 2N2).

13 Bata Shoe Museum

Exploring the sole of history

Like an artsy cousin in the family studying anthropology, the Bata Shoe Museum sits at the same table, Bloor Street West, as the aristocratic uncle, the Royal Ontario Museum. Is this museum a monument to footwear merchandising, or to satiating shoe fetishes à la Carrie Bradshaw? No, it is rather a surprisingly diverse and meticulously curated anthropological experience of world history through shoes. Colour, material, pattern, shape, form and method are present in each artistic display of footwear. Where else could you find menacing looking French chestnut-crushing clogs under the same roof as delicately embroidered Chinese silk shoes, Japanese *fumidawara* rice straw snow boots shaped like elephant legs, and footwear made for exclusively shamanic rituals? And let us not forget the exhibit the next floor up, 'Standing Tall: The Curious History of Men in Heels', from King Louis XIV of France to the neo-peacocking of Ziggy Stardust.

The Bata Shoe Museum is not just a museum, but also a foundation set up by Sonja Bata. The foundation has conducted field research, primarily in the vast Arctic. In this limitless and mysterious land, 'Art and Innovation: Traditional Arctic Footwear from the Bata Shoe Museum' shows us that within thin lines for survival, there is an incredible diversity found in Greenland, Alaska, Northern Canada, Siberia, and Lapland. The lace and colourful beadwork, sealskin, bone and boot designs all bear completely different expressions of the Arctic. Revel in the extraordinary handcrafted skin-work and animal work, lacework, innovative waterproof stitching, dying and treating with oils to create gorgeous, customized footwear encoded with cultural and social meaning.

Visit the world's largest shoe museum, with 1,000 shoes on display and another 14,000 in storage, and look upon your own shoes with a fresh new perspective and appreciation.

Address 327 Bloor Street West, Toronto, Ontario, M5S 1W7, +1 (416)979-7799, www.batashoemuseum.ca | Getting there Subway to St. George (Line 1 & 2) | Hours Mon–Sat 10am–5pm, Sun noon–5pm | Tip If your own shoes have become uncomfortable from walking around the museum, cross the road and visit the Xiaolan Health Centre, one of Toronto's top Chinese wellness centres for massage and acupuncture. Xiaolon Zhao, who runs the Centre, is one of the world's leading authorities on Western use of traditional Chinese medicine (TCM) and is an internationally published author (88 Prince Arthur Avenue, Toronto, ON M5R 1B6, www.xiaolanhealthcentre.com).

14   The Beaches
at the Beaches
Copacabana on the lake

On the sandy shores of Lake Ontario, you'll find Ashbridge's Bay and Woodbine Beach. Woodbine is the westernmost beach in the trendy, upscale neighbourhood of the Beaches. Surprisingly, the Bay was once part of the marshlands east of Toronto Islands and Toronto Harbour until 1912, when the Harbour Commission launched a major scheme to drain and reclaim the land, the largest engineering project in North America at the time. The park opened in 1977, and the bay is surrounded by marinas, playgrounds and an outdoor Olympic-sized pool, complete with a 10-metre diving platform for the brave at heart.

There is a vibrant pulse to the Beaches on hot summer days. Originally a cottage community, it has enjoyed a laid back, youthful vibe for over a century. The cross section of ethnicities, sporting activities and ages make it a melting pot for thousands of Torontonians. Jump on the well-maintained, 56-kilometre / 35-mile Martin Goodman multi-use trail system, or perhaps enjoy a stroll on the 3-kilometre / 1.8-mile boardwalk. The trail beautifully darts in and out of well-protected greenery between the glorious, sandy waterfront and the poetic half-moon curved shoreline.

Interestingly, the sandy beach is proudly home to the largest number of beach volleyball courts in the world, surpassing even Rio! The sheer number of tall, bronzed athletic bodies chasing volleyballs evokes the brash beauty of Copacabana. The sea of 90-plus courts is home to many national tournaments. The options are endless: play volleyball, paddle in the lake or the free city pool, fly a kite, have a picnic, ride your bike, toss a frisbee or walk your dog. Don't forget the sunsets and fireworks and the soft, never-ending sand. Whatever your fancy, Ashbridge's and Woodbine are friendly destinations that are open and accessible to all.

Address 1675 Lake Shore Boulevard East, Toronto, ON M4L 3W6, www.toronto.ca/data/
parks/prd/facilities/complex/1/index.html | Getting there 501 Queen streetcar to Coxwell
Avenue; subway to Coxwell (Line 2) | Hours Unrestricted | Tip The Art Deco-inspired
Harris Water Treatment Plant, better known as the Palace of Purification, is both a crucial
piece of infrastructure and an architecturally acclaimed historic building named after the
long-time commissioner of Toronto's public works R. C. Harris. Although the inside is not
open to the public, the exterior is worth a visit (2701 Queen Street East, Scarborough,
ON M4E 1H4, www.toronto.ca).

15 Berczy Park Dog Fountain

A canine studded fountain and pooch piazza

Move over cat lovers: Toronto has fallen hard for a new canine-studded fountain. Adjacent to St. Lawrence Market is the recently redesigned, revamped Berczy Park, complete with 27 life-sized, cast-iron statues of dogs. This beautiful canine statue sanctuary was the creation of world-renowned Montreal landscape architect Claude Cormier. Cormier, who also designed the playful Sugar Beach, remodelled the park in celebration of the dogs who visit from nearby.

Cormier's unique, whimsical style is present in this massive, three-tier fountain displaying both poetry and humour. The inspiration for the fountain's shape was a dog's collar, lovingly ringed by almost 1,500 stainless-steel studs. Berczy Park is complete with places to perch and lunch, rows of trees, gardens and a magnificent patchwork of granite mosaic. It is not only a green space, but a carefully planned, Italian-inspired piazza. The triangular-shaped park celebrates the playfulness in all of us – water comically spurts out of the dogs' mouths as they peer up towards the mesmerizing golden bone at the top of the fountain. Beagles, Saint Bernards and even the noble household mutt are represented. Not to be forgotten, there is a cat sitting by the edge of the water, admiring two little birds. The feline was added after a woman at a community meeting questioned why the fountain was so dog-centric. If you feel inclined to bring your own furry friend to the park, the lower level of the fountain provides a large water trough. With over 2,000 tail-wagging canine visitors per day, access to water is both a necessity and thoughtful design.

For the downtown core with its oppressive high office buildings, this animated and optimistic park allows for a welcome respite in the middle of a stress-filled working day. The park is open to cat and dog lovers alike, so everyone can enjoy this pooch piazza.

Address 35 Wellington Street East, Toronto, ON M5E 1C6, +1 (416)338-4386, www.toronto.ca/data/parks/prd/facilities/complex/277/index.html | **Getting there** Subway to King (Line 1) then walk 350 meters southeast in the direction of Berczy Park | **Hours** Unrestricted | **Tip** On the eastern tip of the park is the Heritage Gooderham building, also known as the Flatiron building for its wedge shape. Built in 1891 by the Gooderham family, it cost $18,000 and is one of the most photographed buildings in Toronto (49 Wellington Street East, Toronto, ON M5E 1C9, www.historicplaces.ca/en/rep-reg/place-lieu.aspx?id=8311).

16___ The Bergeron Centre

Come float among the engineers

The Bergeron Centre for Engineering Excellence opens your mind to new possibilities and redefines education – perhaps a place to float while exploring new passions and gaining invigorating perspectives? In fact, the building is poetically designed to represent a cloud floating over a rock on Georgian Bay. The facade is made up of a series of 8,000 triangular metal panels and windows positioned according to a complex and precise algorithm, thus evoking the properties of a cloud that is both scale-less and ever changing. Reflecting light and pattern both across the campus and into the building's interior, it is a launch pad for a new breed of renaissance engineers.

The University of Toronto's stately campus has always been well integrated, unlike the more sprawling, disconnected York University, which was laid out in the 1960s. The engineering building gives new life to the campus and a facelift to this suburban plot of land. Taking a page from MIT's Building 20, or the sleek Silicon Valley aesthetic, it emphasizes the importance of mixing disciplines, allowing work to be performed in the open while creating spaces for productivity inside. Learning is reversed as students watch lectures online and come to class to work on projects collectively – new approaches creating new ideas.

Walking through one of the glass doors of 'the Cloud', you are struck by the natural light-filled spaces for collaboration. The halls and staircases are wide. Students are given the brightest spaces, while offices are located in the core. Seating is flexible, ranging from privacy booths to rolling chairs and sofas. Your body is allowed to move with ample space for creative prototyping. Stop by the Sandbox, which includes a 3-D lab, collaboration islands, writeable painted glass and scribble pads. Here, you can explore the future of learning environments and float among the engineers.

Address 4700 Keele Street, 11 Arboretum Lane, North York, ON M3J 1P3, +1 (416)736-5484, www.lassonde.yorku.ca, ask@lassonde.yorku.ca | Hours Unrestricted from the outside | Tip Visit the York University subway station on the recently opened Spadina extension. The station was designed to contribute to the architectural renaissance at the university (120 Ian MacDonald Boulevard, Toronto, ON M3J 1P3).

17 Beth Tzedec's Reuben and Helene Dennis Museum

Take a peak at Canada's largest Judaica collection

Toronto is home to Canada's largest Jewish population. With 200,000 Jewish people residing here, this important ethnic minority has made a profoundly positive impact on the city's history. To better understand Jewish heritage and culture, visit the remarkable Reuben and Helene Dennis Museum, located in the Beth Tzedec Congregation, the largest Jewish congregation in Canada.

Dorion Liebgott is the long time, passionate curator of the museum. Ms. Liebgott gracefully melds both history and modern life into the exhibits. As museum artefacts and displays populate the hallways of the synagogue on route to the museum proper, you begin to understand that this museum is a labour of love. With rotating contemporary shows, such as 'From Latkes to Laffas' about Jewish culinary traditions, a rich history comes alive.

The large one-room museum is very manageable despite housing the largest Canadian Judaica collection. It opened in 1965 with the acquisition of the extensive collection of the renowned Jewish historian and Oxford professor Dr. Cecil Roth, who amassed the cultural objects over a 45-year period. Within the meticulously organized treasury there are so many places to look – a breathtaking collection of items from colourful menorahs, century-old knives for cutting challah bread, a Passover plate from 1673 and a world-famous grouping of ketubots, or Jewish marriage contracts, all celebrating vibrant Jewish traditions. On a more sombre note, there is an original Auschwitz concentration camp uniform and an array of badges identifying people as Jewish from WWII.

For residents and visitors alike, this museum is a first-class, free of charge gem. It is a wonderful way to pass an afternoon and open your eyes to Toronto's important Jewish community and history.

Address 1700 Bathurst Street, Toronto, ON M5P 3K3, +1 (416)781-3514, www.beth-tzedec.org/page/museum | Getting there 7 Bathurst bus to Elderwood Avenue or to Warwick Avenue | Hours Mon, Wed, & Thur 11am–1pm & 2–5pm, Sun 11am–2pm | Tip For an authentic Kosher Jewish experience, try Chicken Nest on Bathurst. It is a deli-style delicious eatery featuring their award winning chicken soup and an eclectic assortment of meats, hearty sandwiches, and salads (3038 Bathurst Street, Toronto, ON M6B 4K2, www.thechickennest.ca).

18 Bloor Viaduct Luminous Veil

A poetic response to tragedy

Spanning 494 metres/0.3 miles and elevated 40 metres/131 feet above the ground and visible at night to thousands of driving, biking and walking commuters a day, the Luminous Veil bridge reveals a special public artwork, designed by Dereck Revington to prevent suicide. Most Torontonians know that the double-decker Bloor Viaduct Bridge crosses the Rosedale Ravine, connecting the city centre to its eastern side. The upper portion is for cars, and just beneath runs the subway. What most Torontonians don't know is that celebrated Canadian author Michael Ondaatje uses the construction phase of this bridge as the setting for *In the Skin of a Lion*. Ondaatje references its architectural features and the workers who died building the bridge around 1917 through illuminating prose.

Unfortunately, 480 suicide deaths have occurred here, making it second only to San Francisco's Golden Gate Bridge for such an ominous distinction. Even more of a morbid consequence is how the bodies would fall onto the busy Don Valley Expressway, creating calamity below. The city was desperate and sought a solution. Revington's submission not only solved the problem, but poetically illuminates an otherwise dark history. Revington would draw inspiration from Ondaatje's story and the human-centred prose of his work, throughout the conception of the *Luminous Veil*. The protective cable barrier is constructed of 9,000 steel rods spaced 12.7 centimetres/5 inches apart and fixed by an angled steel frame. Computer sensors play the installation like an 'elusive Stradivarius instrument' by using the changing wind and temperature data to guide the movement of coloured LED lights. This ever-changing visual display has served as a metaphor to remember those lost lives. Both the bridge and the lights are connectors that honor the bridge's dark story.

Address Bloor Street East / Danforth Avenue, Toronto, ON M4W | Getting there The Luminous Veil spans between Castle Frank and Broadview stations (Line 2) from either station | Hours Unrestricted | Tip Cross the bridge and enter the Danforth area to the east, and go to Allen's, a charming, upscale Irish-inspired pub and eatery decorated in a retro style (143 Danforth Avenue, Toronto, ON M4K 1N2, www.allens.to).

19_Boralia

A delicious bite into Canadian history

When husband and wife team Wayne Morris and Evelyn Wu happened upon a collection of historic recipes from Nova Scotia in an obscure bookstore, the dream of Boralia was sparked. Boralia, or Borealia, was one of the candidates for the nation's name when the Fathers of Confederation created Canada in 1867. This fateful twist in history inspired the husband and wife culinary team, who in turn called their new restaurant Boralia, the Latin term for 'of the North'.

The interior of the restaurant is a mid-century modern interpretation of a native longhouse, tastefully appointed with bundled furs, woodland-themed wallpaper and a life-size carving of an Arctic wolf. Sounds a bit overly iconic, but this collection of Canadiana blends beautifully with the relaxing, mellow charm of a contemporary dining experience.

Many menu items have dates associated with them, such as the top-selling 1605 recipe for mussels smoked in pine needles, dreamed up by explorer Samuel de Champlain. The menu is an historical and cultural mash-up, which reflects Indigenous cuisine, pioneer sensibilities and modern tastes. Imagine Chinese devilled tea eggs, a menu item that was brought here by Chinese immigrants working the Yukon gold rush in 1850. Or cured trout grilled over cedar branches. With menu items such as these, it's easy to appreciate that Wayne Morris spent his youth hunting in New Brunswick, and Evelyn Wu apprenticed under world-famous historian/chef Heston Blumenthal in England.

Such is the Boralian experience: celebrated contemporary chefs digging into our country's past, creating wildly popular dishes, replete with fabulous cocktails. All this bounty is served up in a tastefully nostalgic environment on Ossington Avenue, a newly minted Soho-esque neighbourhood. History has never tasted this good, nor been interpreted with such a modern culinary twist.

Address 59 Ossington Avenue, Toronto, ON M6J 2Y9, +1 (647)351-5100, www.boraliato.com, info@boralieato.com | **Getting there** 501 Queen streetcar to Ossington Avenue | **Hours** Wed–Sun 5:30–10pm | **Tip** Kŭ-kŭm Kitchen is a new Indigenous restaurant that has opened to rave reviews. Check out the authentic vibe from its First Nations Chef Joseph Shawana (581 Mount Pleasant Road, Toronto, ON M4S 2M5, www.kukum-kitchen.com).

20__ The Cameron House
Art incubator concert tavern covered in ants

When wildly popular Emmy Award-winning TV series *Orphan Black* was creating the mood for its main character way back in Season 1, the director chose the Cameron House to film. Why? Well, the Cameron House has invited the edgier elements of the art and music scene through its doors since 1981. It would be appropriate for the director of a sci-fi thriller to pay homage to the home of such avant-garde theatre and film movements such as the Video Cabaret, which is just one of the many artistic movements that came out of the slightly dilapidated corner tavern on Queen Street West.

The Cameron House was purchased by the Ferraro family in 1981, who have run it ever since. While renovating the building, they found beautiful crown molding and floors from a different era. They invited their artist friends (and they had many!) to paint ceiling frescos of baroque/punk angels and cherubs. These angels look down from the ceilings throughout the whole venue, which consists of two separate performance spaces and L shaped bar. It is a vast, artistic mash-up that leaves the first-time visitor in awe.

Outside, the vestiges of a civic protest cling to the exterior of the building. The kooky sculpture of 10 ants crawling across the bricks are known by every regular passerby. The tenant artists who were living upstairs created *Ten Ants* and stuck them there to protest against the city officials who wanted to kick them out of the Cameron House. That visual pun of oversized, white, crawling insects brought them much notoriety and also helped them win over the city officials.

Emerging musicians now carry the torch that lights up this renowned tavern every single night with live music. With the likes of Blue Rodeo and Bare Naked Ladies, who got their start at the Cameron House, these bands will sweep you away with the ever-present indie music tunes and into the arms of a baroque punk angel.

Address 408 Queen Street West, Toronto, ON M5V 2A7, +1 (416)703-0811,
www.thecameron.com, cosmo.ferraro@hotmail.com | Getting there 501 Queen
streetcar to Spadina Avenue; 510 Spadina streetcar to Queen Street | Hours Daily
4pm – 2am | Tip Want to keep it really alternative? Go check out the music a couple of
blocks away at the Bovine Sex Club (542 Queen Street West, Toronto, ON M5V 2B5,
www.bovinesexclub.com).

21 The CAMH Wall

Breaking down walls

Heading down Queen West, you arrive at the new, somewhat stylized, Centre for Addiction and Mental Health (CAMH) urban village, surrounded by fragments of its own heritage wall. The broken down CAMH wall is a perfect metaphor for the changes happening in the world of mental health, namely the growing realization that people with mental illnesses can get better, and the professional consensus that the brain can change itself. The physical walls of this former 'lunatic asylum' are, for the most part, gone. The attitudinal walls supporting the idea that people with mental illness need to be separated from society are crumbling as well.

The Toronto Lunatic Asylum was originally built in 1861 at 999 Queen West. It was the first institution of its kind in the province to care for people who were mentally ill. Prior to this time, those with mental illnesses were typically placed in jails or poor houses. Although these homes were originally seen as a place of refuge and containment, vicious violence became an everyday reality for the patients. The 50-acre property was fully enclosed with a 4,400-linear-foot masonry wall, complete with a trench. Unpaid patient labour was exploited and used almost exclusively during the wall's various construction periods. The remaining wall has been preserved as a memorial to those who lived, worked and died within its confines, never to be remembered with parks or statues. The old stonewall is all that remains. Their stories unfold and are commemorated by nine plaques that examine both the contributions and exploitations of the patients.

As you examine the heritage wall and the CAMH grounds, you may be disturbed by the harsh wall's history there, but rather focus on how much has changed. Given the current flurry of new donations to CAMH, Toronto is aiming for even fewer walls and more positive outcomes for those who suffer from mental illnesses.

Address 1001 Queen Street West, Toronto, ON M6J 1H4, +1 (416)535-8501, www.camh.ca, info@camh.ca | **Getting there** 501 Queen streetcar west to CAMH; subway to Ossington (Line 2), then take the 63 Ossington bus south to Queen Street | **Tip** If you are looking for a coffee or a cocktail, stop in at the Walton – a small Italian gem of a restaurant, in the heart of Little Italy (607 College Street, Toronto, ON M6G 1B5, www.thewalton607.com).

22 Canoeing the Humber River

Paddling Indigenous watercraft

There is no form of transportation as quintessentially Canadian as a canoe. This iconic vessel serves as a unifying symbol across this northern nation. Thus it is both exciting and appropriate that residents and visitors to Toronto are able to navigate outside of their comfort zones and easily access Toronto Adventures, an outdoor recreation company, on the banks of the Humber River.

Located in the city's West End, Toronto Adventures' canoeing experiences are accessible to everyone, and, as their tagline suggests, it is pure 'recreation at your doorstep'. Ted Cordina started the enterprise as a summer hobby but has grown the business with the help of his two sons to include not only summer canoeing, kayaking and camping, but also winter snowshoeing and moose spotting. As the only Humber River canoe and kayak company, it now serves 20,000 adventurers annually.

Although not as quiet and pollution free as her Algonquin Park neighbour, the Humber Valley shares its ability to transport you to a better place. Cast off from the shores, with bridges looming above, and begin to enjoy the slow-moving currents as you float into a paddling paradise. Heading south alongside parklands and bike trails, you pass beautiful homes with private jetties. Aesthetics range from gritty, urban decay and graffiti murals to hidden, magical marshes and abundant wildlife. With osprey, cormorants, kingfishers, egrets, swans and even the occasional turtle and coyote, you question why anyone would bother to travel to the far north to experience such wonders.

Although a guided tour is available, beginners are able to navigate the shallow waters after a few quick instructions. All is quiet on the river. Turning around at the Humber River Bridge at roughly two hours round-trip, you'll have put in a glorious day's work, paddling and relaxing in this graceful, Indigenous watercraft.

Address Toronto Adventures, 9 Old Mill Road, Etobicoke, ON M8X 0A5, +1 (416)536-2067, www.torontoadventures.ca, info@torontoadventures.ca | **Getting there** Subway to Old Mill (Line 2) | **Hours** Mon–Fri 10am–8pm, Sat & Sun 9am–8pm | **Tip** Adjacent to the canoeing venue, is the Old Mill Toronto, a heritage boutique hotel and spa. After so much paddling, relax with a facial, massage, and a fabulous meal (21 Old Mill Road, Toronto, ON M8X 1G5, www.oldmilltoronto.com).

23 Carousel Bakery

Peameal bacon sandwich celebrates Hogtown's legacy

Where is the first food stop for chef and TV host Anthony Bourdain when he visits Toronto, a city that was once slanderously known as 'Hogtown'? It would be Carousel Bakery, in the St. Lawrence Market, to savour a peameal bacon sandwich, the city's signature sandwich, like the Philly Cheese Steak Sandwich in Philadelphia, the Po-Boy in New Orleans, or the Reuben in New York City.

In 1854, William Davies immigrated to Canada from England and started selling cured hams and bacon at the St. Lawrence Market. Back then, other, less prosperous Ontario towns used the 'Hogtown' moniker maliciously, but it actually was inspired by Toronto's sprawling stockyards and meatpackers. Davies quickly realized that he could export this quality meat to England. He expanded his pork business to such a magnitude that by the late 1800s, his company was the largest supplier of pork in the British Empire. But the question was, how to preserve the pork as it journeyed by land and sea? The solution was found in 1875, when his butchers rolled the cured pork loin in ground yellow peas. *Eureka!* Peameal bacon was born. Eventually, the ground peameal was replaced by a bright yellow coarse cornmeal, which is used to this day.

The peameal bacon sandwich is strictly a Toronto invention. Written up in *The New York Times* on several occasions, the sandwich has also been featured on television in England, Ireland, Japan, Germany, Israel and the US. How's that for international reputation?

Although delicious in all seasons, this famous sandwich is the perfect antidote to warm your insides when the frigid northwest winds blow in the winter. As you line up with other peameal bacon aficionados, Robert Biancolin, the owner of Carousel Bakery and market ambassador, will be happy to give you an overview of meat history and how it had a profound economic effect on all of Toronto.

Address St. Lawrence Market, 93 Front Street East, Toronto, ON M5E 1C3, +1 (416)363-4247, www.stlawrencemarket.com/vendors/vendor_detail/56 | Getting there Subway to Union (Line 1), then walk east 0.5 kilometres/0.3 miles; 121 Fort York-Esplanade bus to Market Street; 514 Cherry streetcar to Jarvis Street; 501 Queen streetcar to Jarvis Street | Hours Tue–Thu 8am–6pm, Fri 8am–7pm, Sat 5am–5pm | Tip Olympic Cheese Mart, also inside the St. Lawrence Market, has an enormous selection of cheeses from around the world. Sample the olives and explore the crowded shelves of condiments and crackers that compliment the cheeses (93 Front Street East, Toronto, ON M5E 1C3, www.stlawrencemarket.com/vendors/vendor_detail/84).

24_Casa Loma Escape Rooms

Tunnel your way in and out of your imagination

Exploring Casa Loma's conservatory and other sun-drenched rooms above ground is a well-known and beautiful experience in Toronto's only castle. Going down into the tunnels and losing touch with the outside world is quite another, one which allows you to plunge into the darkest corners of the castle and its subterranean secrets.

Imagine exploring the nefarious world of Rocco Perri, Ontario's King of the Bootleggers, as he is trying to smuggle whiskey and escape the eye of the law. This story, and many others, has been developed into an immersive escape game played out in the cavernous tunnels and basement rooms of the castle. Rooms are decorated in Prohibition-era style, and elaborately staged set designs hold clues revealing the answers for your ultimate escape. Along the way, actors who play Rocco's wife, bodyguard, crooked cop and fellow villains provide various clues and bring to life the story in an interactive and dramatic way. You are transformed into one of the characters as you investigate and try to unravel the answers necessary to solving the mysteries surrounding your plight.

In a race against time, each new clue and ensuing discovery makes for an exhilarating experience. The actors, with their authentic gangster charm, make sure that the escape room drama remains exhilarating as opposed to frustrating. You'll have only a 16 percent chance at escaping successfully and ending up across the street in what used to be the Casa Loma stables. But not escaping is fun too.

Secret City Adventures, part of the Liberty Group, is actively transforming the Casa Loma experience for Torontonians by bringing new life to a city icon. They have designed the escape rooms so that you are able to explore areas of the castle that have never been open to the public. Bring a group of friends or go solo, and immerse yourself into the darker side of Ontario's history.

Address 1 Austin Terrace, Toronto, ON M5R 1X8, +1 (647)243-7658, www.escapecasaloma.com, casaloma@secretcityadventures.com | Getting there Subway to Dupont (Line 1) | Hours Daily, by appointment only | Tip If you want to continue the mood from days of yore, check out BlueBlood Steakhouse inside Casa Loma. Dark wood, massive booths and dim lighting create an opulent, elegant, classic steakhouse environment (1 Austin Terrace, Toronto, ON M5R 1X8, www.bluebloodsteakhouse.com).

25 Centre Ice at Loblaws
Maple Leaf Gardens in aisle 25

Maple Leaf Gardens is Toronto's most historic hockey landmark. As the home to the beloved Toronto Maple Leafs hockey team from 1931 to 1999, this present-day grocery store was once Toronto's temple to professional hockey, our unwavering national sport. When the Maple Leafs moved to the Air Canada Centre, there was an emotional debate around what would become of this building and its embedded hockey soul. At one point in the city's development, there was a strong possibility that it was to be torn down. After sitting empty for over a decade, the building was turned into a grocery store in 2011, thanks to the deep pockets and vision of Loblaws' Galen Weston and his corporate crew. What has evolved is not so much a grocery store, but rather a market experience for the senses with an overlay of hockey greatness.

Where to begin your hockey journey and where to point your grocery cart is somewhat daunting. The expanse of a multi-coloured cupcake case, an 18-foot wall of cheese and a delicious display of Nutella pizzas turn you quickly into a Pavlovian experiment. Cravings and calories seem to skate deliciously from the many elaborate exhibits and into your cart. Hockey memorabilia is integrated into the entire shopping experience. The huge Maple Leaf statue made of well-worn seats from the former Gardens greets shoppers at the entrance. The bright, shiny orange flooring makes shoppers feel like hockey heroes gliding effortlessly between the aisles.

Set your course and your cart to where Centre Ice awaits: Aisle 25. On opening day at Loblaws in 2011, more than 300 hockey fans lined up to be the first ones to see the iconic red dot once again. And now it's your turn to lace up your imaginary skates and prepare to step into legendary Toronto hockey history on this very spot where everyone from Syl Apps to Darryl Sittler faced off. Welcome to hockey in Canada.

Address 60 Carlton Street, Toronto, ON M5B 1J2, +1 (416)513-6154, www.loblaws.ca |
Getting there Subway to College (Line 1); 506 Carlton streetcar to Church Street |
Hours Daily 7am–11pm | Tip Venture next door and visit the Mattamy Athletic Centre
(50 Carlton Street, Toronto, ON M5B 1J2, www.mattamyathleticcentre.ca). Both on the
main floor and upstairs are artefacts celebrating the Men in Blue of Toronto's beloved
Maple Leafs hockey team.

26_ The Chefs' House

Moving beyond the theoretical

Nestled on the corner of King and Frederick Streets is an historic, red-brick building with a sophisticated, modern overtone, home to the Chefs' House, a student-run restaurant that is an integral part of the culinary program at the George Brown Chef School. Popular amongst locals in the area, it is a hidden gastronomic treasure. The first of its kind in Canada, it is a full-time restaurant, where students are given the opportunity to move beyond the theoretical and acquire real-world culinary skills. Prominent cooking schools like the Culinary Institute of America and Le Cordon Bleu have now successfully adopted the Chefs' House restaurant model. The restaurant reopens itself and reinvents its menu every seven weeks, and students may choose to work in the back or front of the house.

Come inside where large modern windows are elegantly framed between brick pillars, giving this bistro-style fare a true mix of both a fine dining experience and a learning lab eatery. Relaxed but sophisticated, it was recently remodeled in 2014. The second floor is used as a classroom and for events, the third floor is a wine lab and the fourth a test kitchen open to the school, outside groups and corporations.

The prices are unbeatable. At a mere $20 for both an appetizer and main course, your pocketbook is spared. The food is beautifully prepared, and creatively plated, and the service is first class, with students helping through every step. No one is surly, and there is a supportive and relaxed attitude – the young smiles are abundant. George Brown's professors, or better referred to as 'food technicians', carefully watch to ensure that the most important ingredient, learning, is added to each move and each food moment. Relax into your meal, and open your heart and mind, as these talented young students earnestly deliver a fabulous dining adventure.

Address 215 King Street East, Toronto, ON M5A 1J9, +1 (416)415-2260, www.thechefshouse.com, chefshouse@georgebrown.ca | **Getting there** 514 Cherry streetcar east to King Street East at Sherbourne Street; 121 Fort York–Esplanade bus to The Esplanade at Frederick Street | **Hours** Lunch Mon–Fri 11:30am–1:30pm, dinner 6pm with last seating at 8pm | **Tip** Stop by St. James Cathedral for a close-up look at one of the city's oldest churches, established in 1797 (65 Church Street, Toronto, ON M5C 2E9, www.stjamescathedral.ca).

27 ___ Cherry Beach

From billy clubs to butterflies

This sandy stretch has a notorious history that has been washed away over time so as to make this a hidden gem on the southernmost tip of Toronto proper. Urban legend claims that cops would rough up arrested culprits on this isolated, gritty beach. Fear not though. Today, you don't need to be escorted in the back of a cop cruiser to reach this recreational destination.

From these seedy beginnings, Cherry Beach has now become Toronto's best secret beach. A place of lakeside freedom for people and canines alike, it has become a picturesque location to relax, explore, spread, and play or watch aquatic sports. Surrounded by one of North America's largest wetlands, it's a prime location for spotting migrating birds, nesting waterfowl and monarch butterflies. It's also a piece of urban paradise for picnics and BBQs, rowers and kite / wind surfers who relish the protected harbours and lack of people. And for dogs, their designated area is off-leash nirvana.

Face south, and you'll see Leslie Spit. Turn in another direction and see the eastern tip of the Toronto Islands. Gaze north and you will have a unique and astounding view of the downtown Toronto core, and yet another eastward glance for a view of a virgin beach shoreline. It attracts artists and photographers at any time of day, intrepid urban explorers, cyclists and hikers who take a break from the Martin Goodman Trail and people who want to relax and walk on a beach.

Cherry Beach is a must-visit destination for anyone who really wants to witness a sense of place and how the city has interacted with its shoreline. Development will likely be fast and furious around this nugget in the next few years; hopefully, though, Cherry Beach will remain a Blue Flag Award-winning treasure. The beach has cleansed itself of its nefarious past, so hopefully the future will still hold its new reputation as a lakeside sanctuary.

Address 275 Unwin Avenue, Toronto, ON M5H 2N2, www.toronto.ca | Getting there
Subway to Union (Line 1), then walk to Bay Street at Front Street West, and take
72 Pape bus to Commissioners Street at Cherry Street | Hours Daily 6am–11:59pm |
Tip Show up with friends for events at Cherry Beach hosted by Promise, where, on
warm nights during the summertime, weekly electronic dance festivals are happening,
with the musical mixing of such luminaries as Skrillex and Zedds Dedd. Family
friendly, it runs from afternoon to evening (www.ilovepromise.com).

28__ Choir!Choir!Choir!

Joining voices into one heartfelt song

Over six years ago, when Nobu Adelman and Daveed Goldman began to assemble a loosely knit choir, they'd rehearse in a downtown real estate office or in Nobu's living room. From these humble beginnings, the group that has now become Choir!Choir!Choir! (C!C!C!) has been catapulted onto the world stage, including gigs at Carnegie Hall, Radio City Music Hall, and enormous Toronto concert venues.

If you have always wanted to sing, and not just in your shower, this is your opportunity. Anyone who wishes to attend a rehearsal can perform as part of the choir. The only prerequisite is that you sing not only with your lungs, but with your heart. Goldman and Adelman teach the song's arrangement, which will eventually culminate in a live performance. Meetings take place twice weekly in the back room of Clinton's Tavern, and the cost is $5. Every session is recorded as a video or audio clip to share with family and friends.

When Patti Smith performed in Toronto 2013, she heard about C!C!C! after seeing a video clip of the choir performing one of her songs. She was astonished and insisted that C!C!C! perform with her. That was the beginning of their meteoric rise. Their version of David Bowie's 'Space Oddity' performed a week after the musician's death went viral and lead to bookings in New York and other places in Canada and the United States.

The repertoire is expansive, and they often perform with famous Canadian guest artists. Their songs also commemorate the passing of superstars such as Tom Petty, Leonard Cohen and Gord Downie of the Tragically Hip. Recently, the C!C!C! used their new-found fame as a platform for philanthropy. They have raised funds for Indigenous rights in Canada and provided financial aid to Syrian refugees.

As Daveed Goldman says, "It's more than just singing. It's challenging, engaging, emotionally investing, and being proud to be part of something."

Address Clinton's Tavern, 693 Bloor Street West, Toronto, ON M6G 1L5, +1 (416)535-9541, www.choirchoirchoir.com | Getting there Subway to Christie (Line 2) | Hours See website for events schedule, mostly on Tue & Wed | Tip If it's a Monday, go visit Sneeky Dees for locally grown fare, save for the avocados and tomatoes, and for their karaoke nights (431 College Street, Toronto, ON M5T, www.sneaky-dees.com).

29 Christie Pits Tobogganing

Mr. Christie, you make good toboggan hills

The only thing that is as delicious as a good cookie for a child is a great park. And so it is appropriate that Christie Pits Park is named after William Christie, the cofounder of the Christie and Brown Cookie Company. Although the park has gone by other names, it was named after Mr. Christie and his 'good cookies' in 1983. This grassy park is over 20 acres, split evenly between sports fields and grassy picnic areas. The deeply sloped sides of the Pit result in most of the park area sitting well below street level – an attractive geographical feature, but, more importantly, a perfect landscape for any avid tobogganer.

Christie Pits is known to its local residents to be the best sledding hill in the city centre. Grab your toque and toboggan, a traditional form of transport used by the Innu and Cree of northern Canada, and liven up a loathsome winter day. The park sits on the boundaries of the Annex, Bloorcourt and Koreatown, making it a true community mash-up. It is hard to imagine that these fabulous toboggan hills were once the scene of a six-hour riot in August of 1933 between two gangs – one known as the Anglo-Canadian Pit Gang and the other group composed predominantly of young men from Jewish, Italian and Ukrainian backgrounds. When a softball game between the two amateur teams went sideways, sparked on by displays of swastikas, it resulted in a gathering of 10,000 citizens. Scores were injured in what was one of the worst racial incidents ever seen in the city.

Today, it is a community centre of sorts, with an inclusive, informal vibe for both beginners and sledding aficionados alike. Head to the hill just east of the skating rink on the north side. It has the steepest slopes and will most certainly be the busiest. If you're looking for a more relaxing ride, though, try the southern tracks of the Pits. You'll feel cozy within its confines.

Address 750 Bloor Street West and Christie Street, Toronto, ON M6G 3K4, +1 (416)338-4386, www.toronto.ca | Getting there Subway to Christie (Line 2) | Hours Unrestricted | Tip Peperonata Lane can be found just south of Christie Pits on the west side of Bickford Park. Peperonata is an Italian dish of slow-cooked bell peppers, onions and garlic, and the lane got its name because one of the residents on the street has a yearly tradition of cooking the dish in their garage for family, friends and neighbours. As you walk down the alley, an outdoor art gallery awaits. Almost all of the garage doors have been painted with gorgeous, colourful murals (Peperonata Lane, Toronto, ON M6G).

30__Cinecycle

Underground movies, bike repair, and coffee

Martin Heath, the founder of Cinecycle is a unique individual who has been able to combine his two passions under one roof. And where is this roof? It is found down an obscure, almost hidden alley off of one of Toronto's busiest streets. Walking down the gravel laneway, you come to a coach house with an old, weather-beaten, green metal door. You know you've arrived, when you see the tongue and cheek slogan 'Cinecycle Work to Rule' boldly spray-painted on the exterior.

By day, Cinecycle is a bicycle repair shop. This is the ICU of bicycle repair, and Martin is known for fixing the most challenging of cases. On nights and weekends, it transforms into a small cinema venue for hire. Bicycles are moved to the side, rows of comfortable cinema seats are arranged into aisles and the cashier counter becomes a coffee bar.

Martin Heath has been committed to cinema and cycling ever since he was a teenager in England. Recently, he won an award for long-distance cycling in Europe. Cinema was what brought Martin to Canada, when he followed his collaborators with the film *History of Rock and Roll*. Heath started showing independent films during summer festivals around Canada in a large, inflatable cinema. He has worked as a film-print handler and projectionist for many notable organizations in London and Toronto, including what is now known as TIFF (Toronto International Film Festival) for 32 years (see ch. 98).

The repertoire of Cinecycle is eclectic; 16-mm features and shorts, as well as Canadian independent experimental animations are part of the unusual offerings every second Friday of the month. Heath has consistently supported local artists and filmmakers by providing this hidden venue to showcase their work. He is a part of a larger artist's collective called 401 Richmond and took part during the early days when it was set up as a visionary cultural workspace.

Address 129 Spadina Avenue, Toronto, ON M5A 1J7, +1 (416)971-4273, www.super8porter.ca, info@super8porter.ca | Getting there 514 Spadina streetcar to Queen Street; 501 Queen streetcar to Spadina Avenue | Hours See website for movies and events schedule; bike repair is by appointment | Tip Forget the limitations of streaming services and visit Toronto's largest destination video store, Bay Street Video. Choose from a phenomenal selection of DVDs (1172 Bay Street, Toronto, ON M5S 2B4, www.baystreetvideo.com).

31 _ Cinesphere
Birthplace of the IMAX experience

The Ontario Place Cinesphere has danced in the imagination of Torontonians who, in the '70s and '80s would enjoy the world's first IMAX theatre experience. Lining up on elevated ramps that hung over Lake Ontario, crowds would wait outside the domed structure to see what the newest film experience could deliver. IMAX technology, developed here and now found in theatres worldwide, was the early predecessor of virtual reality technology.

Eberhard Zeidler, architect extraordinaire, designed the Buckminster Fuller-inspired Cinesphere as a showpiece in the larger development of Ontario Place. This park and entertainment complex opened on the lakeshore in 1971, four years after Montreal's World Expo, as Ontario's vision of bold futurism designed for public enjoyment. Graeme Ferguson's *North of Superior* was screened for the grand opening, the first film shot on 70-mm film (nine times the size of regular film) and projected on the newly constructed 60-by-80-foot, curved IMAX screen.

Provincial funding to support Ontario Place disintegrated, and the park fell into neglect. The Cinesphere was shut, and the proprietary large-format projection system became an American company. Various visions for the park were proposed, including former Mayor Rob Ford's casino makeover.

As part of the revitalization of Toronto's harbourfront, Ontario Place and the Cinesphere have been brought back to life. The IMAX technology has been revamped with a new laser projection system using 80 million mirrors, enhanced sound system, and seating for over 600. Reopened in the fall of 2017 during Toronto's International Film Festival, the Cinesphere, surrounding facilities and park hold new promise with this freshly polished jewel. For an astounding, all-enveloping cinematic experience, go to this geodesic dome that gave birth to the transporting IMAX experience.

Address 955 Lake Shore Boulevard West, Toronto, ON M6K 3B9, +1 (416)314-9900, www.ontarioplace.com/en/cinesphere, info@ontarioplace.com | Getting there Driving from the east along the Gardiner Expressway West, exit Lake Shore Boulevard, then travel west along Lake Shore Boulevard until you reach Ontario Place Cinesphere. Coming from the west along the Gardiner Expressway West, take Jameson Avenue exit, then continue east on Lake Shore Boulevard, off the Martin Goodman Trail. | Hours Tue–Sun 1–7:30pm, Fri & Sat 1–8:30pm | Tip Check out the palatial grounds of the Canadian National Exposition, affectionately known as 'The Ex', which features various large-format shows throughout the year (210 Princes' Boulevard, Toronto, ON M6K 3C3, www.theex.com).

32 Crazy Dollhouse
Welcome to the land of misfit toys

Surprisingly situated on a quaint, residential Leslieville street is one of the most uniquely decorated homes and gardens in Toronto. Although some may call this dwelling frivolous or tacky, others would argue, perhaps more accurately, that the house and its gardens are exuberantly joyful and creatively bedazzled. Complete with Disney characters, Winnie the Pooh, magical mermaids, and brilliant action figures, it all comes together to create an original garden with a fairytale patina. Changing seasonally, the toy garden comes alive as chimes melodically play, flags fly, and toys swing in the seasonal winds.

Shirley Sumaisar and her son James, who mischievously prefer to call themselves Shirley Temple and James Bond, own the home. Shirley and her husband immigrated to Toronto in 1984 and shortly thereafter acquired the house. After Shirley's husband's death, she decided she would begin to dress up the house in part as a shrine to her late husband but also as a joyful gift to those around her, especially children. In 2006, she was the proud winner of Toronto's Best Small Garden Award, a $200 honour she had bestowed upon her by then Mayor Barbara Hall. Signs are planted and hung throughout the garden with adoring comments about teachers and poignant life lessons, bringing a deeper meaning to the playful oasis.

Take time to examine this creative landscape closely; perchance there is more to this land of misfit toys. Shirley describes how she gratefully accepts toy donations from passerbys. Maybe a chance to allow cast-off toys to dance a little longer or a new organizational tool to combat toy overload? Turning around slowly, you wonder if the M&M characters and faded Flintstone figurines are up to some magical mischief. Upon departure, you are left smiling and questioning not why this playful home exists but why we do not have more like them.

Address 37 Bertmount Avenue, Toronto, ON M4M 2X8 | **Getting there** 501 Queen streetcar to Caroline Avenue | **Hours** Unrestricted from the outside only | **Tip** Maple Leaf Tavern is a new take on an old school Toronto tavern. Full of maple leaf iconography, it is a popular spot for elevated comfort food (955 Gerrard Street East, Toronto, ON M4M 1Z4, www.mapleleaftavern.ca).

33 Curiosa: Purveyors of Extraordinary Things

A perfect mix of magic and experiential retail

With the rise of Amazon Prime and the amazing ability to receive packages in the flash of an eye, one wonders if retail shops, as we know them, will continue. One shop, Curiosa: Purveyors of Extraordinary Things, has found a way to thrive in this uncertain environment and move ahead of the retail curve.

Located on the Queen Street strip in a gentrified part of Parkdale, is a wonderful, well-stocked magic store with a hat tip to Harry Potter. The space is a new take on experiential shopping: destination retail. Shopping here is an adventure, which is just as important as the products that you see on display. Although Curiosa is filled with wondrous objects from the Harry Potter world, the shop is much, much more. It is a place of magic. Founders and owners Steven and Heather Sauer, a husband and wife duo, come from a robust retail pedigree. They own another Toronto gem, the Paper Place. Both shops are true labours of love, and the Sauers have thought through every detail.

Entering into the mysterious shop, you immediately understand you've arrived at an alternative universe with a welcoming, mystical atmosphere. You have been captured by a magical spell. With a gold-leaf celestial clock shining from the ceiling and dark coloured shelves full of interesting artefacts, you are uncertain where to begin. As you make your way through Toronto's Diagon Alley, take note of wand permits, a trick box that cannot be opened, beautiful list books for tracking your enemies, self-stirring cauldrons and mystical board games. If you want to be chosen for one of Hogwart's houses, you can create a good luck token coloured for your newly assigned mascot. Make sure not to miss the MinaLima prints, including originals from the creators of the stunning graphic design team who specialize in Potter on-screen adaptations.

Address 1273 Queen Street West, Toronto, ON M6K 1L6, +1 (647)341-0394, www.curiosasociety.com, orders@curiosasociety.com | **Getting there** 501 Queen streetcar to Brock Avenue; 29 Dufferin bus to Dufferin Street | **Hours** Mon–Fri 11am–7pm, Sat 10am–6pm, Sun noon–5pm | **Tip** Be sure not to miss the Harry Potter-inspired Lockhart Cocktail Bar. This cozy, exposed-brick haunt conjures up cocktails and tapas (1479 Dundas Street West, Toronto, ON M6J 1Y8, www.thelockhart.ca).

34 Doll Factory By Damzels

Girls just want to have fun frocks and more…

Doll Factory by Damzels, a small store on Queen Street East, weaves fun, nostalgic fashion and accessible design into the retail scene in Leslieville. This fashion/passion creation of Rory Lindo and Kelly Freeman opened up in 1994. The partners had met in college over 20 years ago, when they had their sewing machines next to one another at the George Brown College Fashion Program. One brought a sense of girly, the other a love of rock and roll, and both shared a passion for the vintage aesthetic. They set out to sell their hand-made dresses at open markets and rock festivals. When they opened their store, they hired staff who had been through the 'art house meets fashion' journey with them, and they started garnering attention and awards. The Canadian fashion industry critics believe we now have our version of Betsey Johnson tucked away in Toronto.

It's actually not easy to summon one's inner femme fatale with dresses that are figure flattering and celebrate curves because women are so often hardest on themselves. So it is the job of the sales staff to help women see themselves in a new light and relax into tastefully playful and well-fitted frocks. Take that, Bettie Page! Sizing is accessible, with sizes 0 to 3x, and so is the pricing, with dresses mostly around the 100 dollar mark.

To compliment the dresses, Damzels also sell all sorts of retro and rockabilly items, such as coasters, fridge magnets and plates. A strange pattern has emerged over the years that no one in the store can explain; the boutique is the biggest seller of Burt Reynold naked photo plates in the world. It is hard for Rory and Kelly to keep this dishy dish in stock. Artist and supplier Jim Spinx in Florida cannot decipher why the Damzels are his best customers. Is it our long winters that make that hairy manly man so appealing? Go and see if you can help resolve this long-standing mystery.

Address 1122 Queen Street East, Toronto, ON M4M 1K8, +1 (416)598-0509, www.damzels.com, damzels@damzels.com | **Getting there** 501 Queen streetcar to Caroline Avenue | **Hours** Tue–Sat 11am–6pm, Sun noon–5pm | **Tip** Go visit their other location at the west end of the city, in the vibrant area of Roncesvalles Avenue to get a different and bigger perspective on 'girly meets rock 'n' roll' dressmaking (394 Roncesvalles Avenue, Toronto, ON M6R 2M9).

35 __ The Don Jail

Toronto's grim, gory past

It seems bewildering that one of the most grimacing jails in Canada's history existed in the picturesque neighbourhood of Riverdale. The Don Jail, opened in 1864, was originally seen as a reform prison, dubbed the 'Palace for Prisoners' because of its progressive approaches to inmate wellness. However, over time, its reputation changed. Fuelled by a series of high-profile escape attempts, the Don's notoriety grew, and inquiries found the vermin-infested jail grossly understaffed.

The grand Italian-style building was built to be intimidating, similar to Alcatraz. Thirty-four men were hanged in the jail's gallows, including Canada's last public execution in 1962. The first executions were actually ticketed public spectacles. Canada's most famous hangman, Arthur English, who used the pseudonym 'Arthur Ellis' after a famous English executioner, worked at the jail. However, his career abruptly ended after a botched execution and an accidental beheading.

Observe the image of Father Time above the entrance – a severe reminder to those who arrived in shackles. Although no longer so grim, repainted and void of historic stenches, it still feels ominous. The rotunda, featuring original iron railings and balconies, served as the set for the Cell Block Bar in the movie, *Cocktail*. The gallows have been taken down, although a few cramped cells remain. Don't miss the cigarette burns on the flooring outside the execution chamber – a final pleasure for those unlucky souls.

The jail finally closed in 1977 and over time was converted into administrative offices for Bridgepoint Health. During the renovation, eerie murals and numerous skeletons were discovered. Bridgepoint, a gold standard for long-term and palliative care, is a form of karmic redemption for the Don. Although it's now a fine workplace, you wonder what ghostly villains still linger in the hallways.

Address 550 Gerrard Street East, Toronto, ON M4M | Getting there 506 Carlton streetcar, or 505 Dundas streetcar to Broadview Avenue at Gerrard Street East | Hours Mon–Fri 9am–5pm, now a private office and offers a self-guided tour | Tip Visit Andrea's Gerrard Street Bakery for some of the best-baked goods in Toronto. Try a 4" Chocolate Fudge Layer 'Wee Cake', especially made not to share (635 Gerrard Street East, Toronto, ON M4M 1Y2, www.andreasbakery635.com).

36 __ Dufferin Grove Skating Rink

Don your toque and grab your skates

Canadians view ice skating as a right of passage, like swimming is to some nations, a required skill for children and adults alike. Despite Canada's long winter, residents across this northern nation are able to pluck themselves from hibernation, don their toques and shiny blades and head out for regular ice-skating experiences. Toronto celebrates its Canadian spirit and prides itself in having more outdoor artificial ice rinks than any other city in the world. In the early 1950s, however, there were only six outdoor rinks in Toronto, as opposed to over 50 today. Dufferin Grove Skating Rink is a fabulous five-acre, multi-use marvel and is one of Toronto's 'original six'.

All outdoor skating rinks in the city have their own signature – their own mix of skating schedules and accoutrements. The Dufferin Rinks seems to have thought through these important elements more creatively and carefully. With skate and helmet rentals totalling just a *toonie,* it is an absolutely affordable and accessible activity. As you enter into the well-loved clubhouse, you are greeted by many red-cheeked, smiling faces – a welcome melting pot of ages, nationalities and, most certainly, skating abilities. With lots of places to perch, you are almost guaranteed to spark up a conversation with your sporty neighbours. Now lace up and get your skating groove going.

The inviting Zamboni Café is a differentiator in the world of skating rinks. Serving organic coffee, hot chocolate and deliciously fresh snacks all at a reasonable price, the café is so inviting that you might just stay there for a while. The two large skating pads that await you are well lit and well supervised. You'll hear a mix of music for all tastes, so don't be surprised if a catchy salsa adds a Latin twist to your glide. Consider warming up post-skate at one of the outdoor bonfire pits.

Address 875 Dufferin Street, Toronto, ON M6H 4B2, +1 (416)392-0913, www.cityrinks.ca, dufferinepark@gmail.com | **Getting there** Subway to Dufferin (Line 2) | **Hours** See website for seasonal hours | **Tip** Looking for a more urban skating experience? Try the Bentway Skate Trail, located under the Gardiner Expressway, right by the Fort York Visitor Centre. Glide along the 220-metre / 700-foot figure-8 loops between the big columns, or bents, that hold up the Gardiner Expressway (250 Fort York Boulevard, Toronto, ON M5V 3K9, www.thebentway.ca).

37 Earth Echoes

Come visit this lizardly lair

It is intriguing that someone would dedicate their life's work to nurturing, breeding and selling reptiles. The calm and peaceful Paul Collier, nicknamed the 'Lizard King', is just that person. He is the owner and operator of Earth Echoes, a reptile centre and home to both expert knowledge and the healthiest reptiles, including snakes, lizards, birds, turtles and tortoises, available in Toronto.

Raised in the city, Collier got his start in the reptile business at the tender age of seven. Training his first lizard to sleep under his desk lamp at night, he graduated at the age of 10 to snakes, with funds generated from his paper route. Telling his mother it was a brown mud snake from the Humber River, he got her to enjoy the snake too. This courageous and adaptive woman was somewhat shocked, and likely terrified, when learning that it was actually a boa constrictor.

By the age of 24, Collier began breeding temperamental veiled chameleons, giving him an outstanding reputation within the reptile industry – yes, slightly esoteric yet specialized. The rest is history, as they say, and Collier has bred over 20,000 veiled chameleons in addition to 25 separate species of reptiles to date.

Walking into his midsize store, located at Bloor and Brock Streets, you are amazed that everywhere you turn, there is a new ecosystem. The store, which has been open since 1991, is very lush, with low-lit warming lights. Breathing in, you feel like you might be close to a reptilian den in the rainforest, with a primordial fragrance throughout. At the rear of the store resides a large incubator containing hundreds of lizard, snake and chameleon eggs. Collier believes these reptiles make ideal, civilized and durable city pets. They do not require walks, are inexpensive to feed and demand much less attention than a run-of-the-mill furry friend.

Visit this lizardly lair and ponder adopting a reptilian companion.

Address 1192 Bloor Street West, Toronto, ON M6H 1N2, +1 (416)389-3143, www.earthechoes.ca | Getting there Subway to Dufferin (Line 2) | Hours Daily 2–8pm | Tip If you want to further your reptile experience, visit Reptilia, Canada's largest indoor reptile zoo, with 15,000 square feet of indoor exhibits featuring over 250 reptiles and amphibians. It is located in Vaughan, Ontario (2501 Rutherford Road, Concord, ON L4K 2N6, www.reptilia.org).

38 Edwards Gardens Redwood

Toronto's canopy comes alive with this fossil gem

Despite her thick middle, she's elegant and graceful, and her far-reaching arms seem to draw you in. Her reddish complexion and sheer size invite you to pause and maybe climb on. She is alluring, she is grounding and she is not to be missed. Accessible to all, she is a Dawn Redwood, a magical tree from ancient times and the star of Toronto's Edwards Gardens. Dawn, with her slightly tangled trunk, looks somewhat animated, evoking thoughts of a tree refuge, more reminiscent of the Hobbits' Shire or perhaps even Jurassic Park.

The Dawn Redwood, or *Metasequoia* (literary translation: 'like a Sequoia'), is one of the few of its kind in Toronto and a distant relative of the Californian Sequoias. It is often referred to as a living fossil, a relic from the era of the dinosaurs. It was believed that these trees were extinct until one was found in China in the 1940s. This radiant deciduous conifer found in Edwards Gardens is one of the oldest trees in Canada. Planted in 1960, the tree only seeds every 40 years, highlighting the fragility and importance of this type of tree. This one in Edwards Gardens is carefully positioned on a site painstakingly selected by the gardener who planted it. The gardener selected the specific spot for its optimal lighting, thus assuring that Dawn would be bathed in early morning sunshine on June 20th of each year, the birthday of his wife. Although the years have passed, the tree still stands majestically on the top of a hill, happily thriving amidst the pines and maples, and representing a true testament to the gardener's devotion and creativity.

Although not specifically labeled, it is hard to miss the Dawn Redwood. The sheer size and majesty of this formidable tree will force you to take a second look. Take time to explore Edwards Gardens in its entire splendor and stand in awe of Mother Nature's gift of this fossil gem.

Address 755 Lawrence Avenue East, North York, ON M3C 1P2, +1 (416)397-1340, www.toronto.ca | **Getting there** Subway to Eglinton (Line 1), then take 54 Lawrence East bus to Leslie Street at Lawrence Avenue East; by car, use Don Valley parkway, exit Lawrence Avenue and continue driving west until you reach Edwards Gardens | **Hours** Unrestricted | **Tip** Stop in at the Toronto Botanical Gardens building on the grounds and visit the Garden Café at the barn. The surrounding gardens are designed to educate and inspire, which they certainly do for any budding botanist (777 Lawrence Avenue East, North York, ON M3C 1P2, www.torontobotanicalgarden.ca).

39 _ Elevated Wetlands

Art in the environment

'What's that?' You've just seen a fleeting white flash of sculpted polar bears / molars / topless elephants cross your peripheral vision as you drive on the Don Valley Parkway. Or maybe you are walking on the Taylor Creek Trail, wandering past large white container-like sculptures several stories high, filled with growing deciduous and evergreen trees. Like water pitchers, tipping one into the next, these primal creatures invite you to touch their organic shapes and caress their legs. Or molar roots? Your imagination flows. That is the way the artist, Noel Harding, imagined it, to pose a perpetual question about his creation of the Elevated Wetlands by the Don River.

Today more than ever before, the problems and solutions caused by polluted waters and flooding are part of our national dialogue. In 1996, Noel Harding's artistic concept was to create a 'functioning sculpture,' blending both man-made materials and natural, organic vegetation. Harding also focused on the idea of a sustainable habitat. He took the Canadian Plastic Industry's money and materials to build the three-storey containers, which filter polluted water through recycled plastic 'soil' before returning clean water to the river. Thus, removing pollutants from the environment is a major component to the sculptures, and they are constantly changing visually with the seasons. As any gardener would know with their annual plantings, as the vegetation grows, the focus becomes less about the container, and more about the greenery.

The pioneering work of the late Noel Harding is increasingly being referenced by emerging artists who explore the questions: if art is the experience of perceiving, can it also act as a catalyst for environmental change?

Noel Harding provokes us to ask these types of questions, as we also ask ourselves about what label we wish to give this environmental artwork.

Address Accessed by Taylor Creek Trail, 260 Dawes Road, East York, ON M4C 5M8 | Getting there Bike or walk the Taylor Creek Trail (just south of the Don Mills/Don Valley cloverleaf); by car, from downtown, take the Don Valley Expressway north, exit to Don Mills Road and after cloverleaf exits, take a right to drive down to parking area. The sculptures will be on your right. | Hours Unrestricted | Tip To further explore the Don River Valley, take out your trail bike and head off to Crothers Woods for some BMX trails. Entrance is from the Leaside Loblaws (www.trailforks.com/region/crothers-woods-18708/map).

40___Evergreen Brickworks
Where bricks and nature build cities

As the famed journalist Robert Fulford wrote, 'The ravines are to Toronto like what the canals are to Venice.' And at the gateway of the Toronto ravine network sits Evergreen Brick Works, an internationally acclaimed centre of innovation known for its mission supporting the design of sustainable cities. The Brick Works is a massive, former brick-making facility, complete with 19th-century industrial machines and an adjacent 40-acre quarry park, where, for over a 100 years, the bricks were made for Casa Loma, Massey Hall, University of Toronto, Queen's Park and more than 50,000 homes. The clay and bricks from here arguably created the architectural identity of Toronto. For decades, it sat empty, until the city handed over this corroded and eroded liability to a national charity led by visionary entrepreneur Geoff Cape. He, along with his team at Evergreen, used the raw force of unpredictable nature as the foundation and inspiration for every facet of the venue's development and programming. 'Bring it in, and bring it on,' says Cape.

You will see a symbiotic relationship between buildings and nature. As with Dutch dam building, or Louisiana levees, city planners have long attempted to push back, groom and control nature. The Brick Works is teaching us how to develop a new urban planning model that welcomes a partnership with nature. Growing gardens inside the ruinous industrial-era buildings re-establishes this cohabitation. This model is taken even further with the development of the Weston Family Quarry Garden, where draining water becomes a featured element to the marshland beside the industrial buildings.

World leaders and dignitaries visit the site to be inspired by new ways of thinking about our cities' relationships with nature. But anyone can come and enjoy this dynamic public space in the heart of Toronto's ravine systems.

Address 550 Bayview Avenue, Toronto, ON M4W 3X8, +1 (416)596-7670, www.evergreen.ca, info@evergreen.ca | **Getting there** Subway to Davisville (Line 1), then take 28 Bayview South bus, or subway to Broadview (Line 2), and walk to Erindale Avenue to take Evergreen shuttle bus (free) | **Hours** Daily 10am–5pm | **Tip** Bring your skates in the wintertime, and glide around the landscaped islands inside the industrial buildings (www.evergreen.ca/blog/entry/top-10-things-at-evergreen-brick-works/).

41 First Toronto Post Office

Sealed with a kiss – and red wax

With the emergence of the Internet and its resulting email, Twitter and plethora of content sites, there has been a slow strangulation of the postal village as we know it. Beautiful, handwritten notes and post offices have succumbed to the irresistible force of the online world.

Taking us back in time to the buildings at Adelaide and George Streets, is the First Toronto Post Office, otherwise known as Fourth York Post Office. Enter the Georgian, red-brick style building, now operating as a museum, national historical site and post office. In the 1830s when the post office first opened, Canada did not have its own postal system; the mail was controlled by England. This remote British colony was isolated, and the post office was vital for homesick York residents as a connection to the outside world. It was the commercial and social centre for the Town of York, providing the only way to move communications and money.

The full-scale model of the old town of York in the back room of the post office makes an ideal starting point for exploring historic Toronto. Take note of the portraits of J. S. Howard, the first postmaster. Although a Methodist, as opposed to an Anglican, his reputation for integrity earned him the esteemed position. The reading room was where people opened and read their mail. With over 30% of the population under 16 and many unable to read, a staff member would read letters and write replies for patrons.

At a 19th-century table, grab a goose feather and write a letter to a special someone similar to the denizens of times past. For a pittance, you can create a personalized expression full of sentiment. Folding the paper like a magical piece of origami, you seal the letter with a kiss – or a bright red sealing-wax stamp. Hold it carefully so as not to smudge it, and hand it to the smiling staff. The charm of an actual letter is sure to delight.

Address 260 Adelaide Street East, Toronto, ON M5A 1N1, +1 (416)865-1833,
www.townofyork.com, info@tos1stpo.com | Getting there 504 King streetcar, or 514 Cherry
streetcar to King Street West at Jarvis Street; 121 Fort York–Esplanade bus to Frederick
Street | Hours Mon–Fri 9am–5:30pm, Sat & Sun noon–4pm | Tip Built in 1911, Riverside
Bridge links downtown Toronto to the Riverside neighbourhood on the east side of the city.
View the art installation called Time: and a Clock, which includes the inscription 'This river
I step in is not the river I stand in.' (www.riverside-to.com/about/bridge).

42 Forbes Wild Foods

Bringing the bounty of wilderness to the city

Foraged foods have become all the rage with prominent chefs around the world. Chefs use the hand-harvested food repertoire to create new menu items for customers and critics alike. Instead of using olives to garnish a martini, how about using the humble spruce tip? Or how about some birch syrup to glaze trout? At Forbes Wild Foods, there are 150 different foraged foods found in the Canadian wilderness, ready for urbanites to come to the store and select unique ingredients.

Jonathan Forbes and his son Dyson have salvaged an age-old tradition in Canada and made it into a viable commercial operation. Just like the pioneers who came to the New World and had to learn from the Indigenous people, Jonathan's ancestors in Northern Ontario learned to forage from Six Nations communities. In fact, pickers usually live in rural and remote areas of Canada and supply Jonathan with a variety of foods, which may include wild mushrooms, leeks, fiddleheads, wild ginger, cattails and wild chokeberries. All of the foragers who provide Forbes Wild Foods with product are knowledgeable and sensitive to the forest environment so as to maintain a sustainable ecosystem. For example, they know that if a forest is clear cut, mushrooms will not grow for 50–100 years. For this and other reasons, Forbes is on a mission. Jonathan believes, 'People would pay more attention to the environment if they had a relationship with it through food.'

Forbes Wild Foods sells to restaurants, farmers' markets, hotels, health stores and to the public. Come to the warehouse and walk to the back of the café, where you will find the shop door. Inside this new warehouse space, the shop is quaint with rustic, hand-hewn beams and large inviting windows. You cannot get any more organic than foraged wild foods. Invite the richness and subtleties of nature's bounty into your kitchen and your life.

Address 2 Matilda Avenue, Suite 101, Toronto, ON M1M 1L9, +1 (416)927-9106, www.wildfoods.ca, forbes@wildfoods.ca | **Getting there** 501 Queen streetcar east to Carroll Street | **Hours** Mon−Fri 9:30am−5pm | **Tip** One of Toronto's original destinations for organic foods and natural wellness products, the Big Carrot Complex is well worth a visit (348 Danforth Avenue, Toronto, ON M4K 1N8, www.thebigcarrot.ca).

43 __ Galleria Italia at the AGO

A ship that sets sail through art galleries

Floating at the front of the Art Gallery of Ontario (AGO), the Galleria Italia is one of the most cherished architectural designs by the world-famous architect Frank Gehry. Riding the wave of international acclaim from his design of the Guggenheim Museum Bilbao for contemporary art in Spain a decade before, he was commissioned to create a new presence for the art gallery in his hometown of Toronto. In 2007, following the directives of the AGO Board, Gehry was asked to bring the experience of the gallery closer to the community, unify the exhibit halls and create a beautiful space honouring the Canadian outdoor aesthetic.

Gehry met this tall order with the stunning execution of imposing wood, space and glass in the sculpture hall of Galleria Italia. Linking street to gallery, and gallery to gallery, it is both powerful and intimate at the same time. Stretching a city block, Galleria Italia is 450 feet long and over 50 feet high in places. What makes it intimate is the use of Douglas fir lumber, which is used both structurally and decoratively, embracing the gallery visitor with warmth and welcome. Gehry's use of wood pays homage to our nation's history; in fact, it is Canada's largest public art project to use wood. The curved pillars are reminiscent of a ship's hull and the vessels that brought explorers and waves of immigrants to our shore.

Like modern day Medicis, 24 wealthy Italian-Canadian families banded together, collected and donated 10 million dollars to give the space its name of Galleria Italia. Tony Gagliano, an active AGO board member and one-time chair, made sure each family name is embedded into the wooden arches. It is interesting to note that these names read like a who's who of the developers that built Toronto to its post-WWII grandeur. The beauty of inspired design and exquisite materials would not have escaped these developer families.

Address 317 Dundas Street West, Toronto, ON M5T 1G4, +1 (416)979-6648, www.ago.ca |
Getting there 505 Dundas streetcar to Beverley Street; subway to St. Patrick (Line 1) |
Hours Tue & Thu 10:30am–5pm, Wed & Fri 10:30am–9pm, Sat & Sun 10:30am–5:30pm |
Tip Explore another galleria in the heart of the financial district. The Allen Lambert
Galleria, sometimes described the 'crystal cathedral of commerce', is a lofty, light-filled
space with intertwining steel arches towering overhead (181 Bay Street, Toronto, ON M5J,
wwwallontario.ca/allen-lambert-galleria-crystal-cathedral-of-commerce).

44_ Gallery Grill Hart House

Dining Hogwarts style

Rounding the corner of the oak-trimmed walls of Toronto's own Hogwarts Castle, it is easy to feel as though you have stepped back a century. Hart House is built in the style of a neo-Gothic revival, a 20th-century architectural gem. Walking the corridors paved with Italian travertine, you begin to wonder about the motivations of Vincent Massey when he conceived of this architectural statement as a 22-year-old undergraduate. Designed as a campus hub in the middle of the University of Toronto, it is where young and old come to share friendship – and a hidden dining treasure.

Climbing the stairs, you will sense the gourmet aromas permeating the air. Turning the corner and stepping through a stone portal, you know you have entered the Gallery Grill. This hideaway is imbued with a sense of scholarly pomp: lead windows and vaulted ceilings, dark wood and bold lines. This gravitas is a compelling counterpoint to the liveliness of the menu.

Looking closely at the leaded windows, you are teleported back to a world before iPhones and Google, when young student artists would meticulously paint caricatures of their favourite professors on the panels of the stained-glass windows, a whimsical idea of the young Massey. Look closely at the 21 window illustrations carefully depicting portly professors of the early 20th century.

Though frequented by distinguished alumni, academics and well-heeled literati, the Gallery Grill is just waiting to be discovered by mere mortals, without prohibitive pricing. The loyal clientele has a strong allegiance to the history, the atmosphere and the food. The service fully understands the complexities of the dishes and mixes in gentle humour with formality. The diverse menu ranges from homemade scones to rabbit confit. Ask for a table overlooking the Great Hall, where you may glimpse Professor Dumbledore, or his Canadian doppelgänger.

Address 7 Hart House Circle, Toronto, ON M5S 3H3, +1 (416)978-2445, www.harthouse.ca/gallery-grill, gallerygrill@harthouse.ca | Getting there Subway to Museum (Line 1); 5 Avenue Road bus to Queen's Park Crescent at Hart House; 94 Wellesley bus to Queen's Park Crescent | Hours Café Mon–Fri 8–11am; Lunch Mon–Fri 11:30am–1:30pm; Brunch Sun 11am–1:30pm | Tip Just in front of the Hart House stands the Soldier's Tower, commemorating the fallen soldiers of WWI and WWII from the University of Toronto community. Many hauntings have been reported, including a figure who falls from the tower, but no body is ever found (www.thevarsity.ca/2012/09/10/ghosts-of-campus-past).

45 The Gardiner Museum

No crackpots here, just glazed beauty

Across from the Royal Ontario Museum, a small architectural gem houses ceramics and porcelain, both historic and contemporary, from all corners of the world. The Gardiner Museum is dedicated to all things molded and glazed and elevates the art of ceramics to an astonishing level that may inspire anyone to think more appreciatively of the actual artistry imbued in this sculptural art form. You will find a wide range of pottery, from ancient American vessels and Japanese, Viennese and English decorated porcelain, to Italian Renaissance majolica, as well as the most cutting-edge contemporary ceramic exhibits and installations, which are displayed in these elegantly designed halls of the museum.

The Gardiner Museum is not only a labour of love, but ultimately it came from a story of love between Helen and George Gardiner. George, a business wunderkind, ran the Toronto Stock Exchange and had his own brokerage firm. His deep pockets allowed him and his wife to pursue their mutual passion for collecting ceramics. As George said, he "collected porcelain as others would collect real estate." They lovingly decorated their home until it was overflowing with collectibles. The time came to build a museum for their treasures.

The final renovations were completed in 2006, and the building was cited as one of the most beautiful in Toronto. Replete with a glass elevator, a restaurant and working studios, the museum offers workshops, lectures and tours open to all, as well as world-class sculptural exhibits by some of the great masters, including Picasso, Miro and Chagall.

Seasonal installations attract wide public interest, such as the most famous one, a sculptural interpretation of the 12 Trees of Christmas. The museum takes the concept of ceramics as practical items for kitchens and tables, and elevates the creative discipline to the level of high art that it deserves.

Address 111 Queen's Park, Toronto, ON M5S 2C7, +1 (416)586-8080, www.gardinermuseum.on.ca | Getting there Subway to Museum (Line 1) | Hours Mon–Thu 10am–6pm, Fri 10am–9pm, Sat & Sun 10am–5pm | Tip If looking at beautiful ceramics has made you thirsty for a cup of tea steeped in fine bone china, visit the Windsor Arms Hotel Tea Room. Serving high tea since 1927, they have had time to perfect the art of tea time in this small and enchanting boutique hotel (18 St. Thomas Street, Toronto, ON M5S 3E7, www.windsorarmshotel.com/tearoom).

46 Garrison's Barbershop

Cultivate your hipster beard

Apparently, today's men are seeking to enhance their masculinity by being more flamboyant and expressive with their whiskers. A beard can indeed add to a man's attractiveness and the impression he makes, as long as it's flattering and well kept. Otherwise, facial hair can get out of hand. It seems that in larger more competitive societies, men are feeling the need to stand out even more, and so the important role of whisker experts or gentlemen's barbershops has become paramount.

Embracing a steampunk aesthetic, Garrison's Barbershop is a modern take on the classic service establishments and one of the city's finest. If there is a place to cultivate your hipster beard, this is it. Not far from inner-city parks and the flow of Queen Street West, husband and wife Doug Stewart and Hollis Hopkins recently opened the doors to their business, with a nod to the barbershops of years past. Full of interesting guys with interesting stories, it is a place where men can fraternize in a classically male space with a classically masculine aroma. Sport scores, current events and local news (gossip) seem to involve everyone. The white walls and rustic hardwood floors are accented with plush leather seats, vintage maps, retro men's accessories and a classic spinning light pole. The ambiance cloaks you in a feeling of luxury and the comfort akin to the old chop and shave shops. With a talented team of cutters, you can feel confident in their superior clipper training. Shaves and trims are patiently executed. The layers of warm towels and balms result in a close, smooth shave for even the most epidermally challenged.

There are no blowouts or highlights here, just great haircuts and great conversation. Beer and hot toddies, proudly served during the frigid winter months, come with the price of a haircut or shave. For manly pampering or a clean up, go to Garrison's.

HEY THERE

COME ON OVER AND WE'LL TAKE CARE OF YOU.

$35
CUT
Clippers, scissors, it doesn't matter—our skilled team's got you. Comes with a thorough consult and product styling. (Add Straight Razor $90).

$25
BUZZCUT
The classic, with one length all over and a natural taper along the nape to finish things off.

$20
BEARD TRIM
If you're in between visits and in need, we'll use clippers to get those stragglers, blend those burns and then soften the rest with oil and balm.

$60
STRAIGHT RAZOR
Whether you want that beard shaved or lined out, we'll give hot towels, a straight razor, then condition with premium products. (Add Cut $90).

$25
BOY'S CUT
(Ages 6 - 12): Fret not, whatever we do for you, we can do for the kids.

Address 254 Niagara Street, Toronto, ON M6J 1B9, +1 (416)703-8602, www.garrisons.ca, cutandshave@garrisons.ca | Getting there 514 Cherry streetcar west, or 501 King streetcar west to Niagara Street | Hours Tue & Wed 10am – 7pm, Thu & Fri 11am – 8pm, Sat 10am – 7pm | Tip For anyone with a paper obsession, come and wander into the boutique of all things paper at the Paper Place. It has hands-down the best wrapping paper selection in the city (887 Queen Street West, Toronto, ON M6J 1G5, shop.thepaperplace.ca).

47__Gibraltar Point Lighthouse

Haunted beacon of light

The Gibraltar Point Lighthouse, tucked away on the southwest corner of Toronto Island, was built just before the War of 1812 to guide ships into the harbour. This stony beacon is also the site of one of the oldest hauntings in the city, as the ghost of the first lighthouse keeper has been heard moaning ever since his violent death in January of 1815.

The lighthouse was commissioned in 1808 by John Graves Simcoe, the founder of York, the original name of modern Toronto. It was initially built to be 52 feet high, and in 1832 the height was raised to 82 feet. It is Canada's second-oldest lighthouse and the oldest one on the Great Lakes. When it was first built, it rested on the shores of Toronto Island. But with the accumulation of silt over a century, it presently sits inland. Who knows, as global warming makes the waters rise, whether it will once again grace the island shoreline to remind everyone of drunken soldiers and the bloody outcome of bootlegging in the early 19th century?

As the story goes, J. P. Rademuller, a German immigrant, was the first lighthouse keeper at Gibraltar Point Lighthouse. In addition to his job of lighting the whale-oil lamp at top of the lighthouse, Rademuller decided to brew and sell beer. Two soldiers from York, who possibly had just fought in the Wars of 1812 and 1813, were furious when their beer froze on that January night. They had been duped, and were out for revenge! They killed Rademuller, hacked up his body and buried it just outside the lighthouse. He was never seen again, but George Durnan, the lighthouse keeper in 1908, found an adult human jawbone in a box near the tower. The German bootlegger has been haunting the lighthouse ever since, sending a chill down the spine of many an island visitor.

Address Toronto Island Park, Toronto, ON M5V 2X3, +1 (416)203-6753, www.torontoisland.com | Getting there From the Jack Layton Ferry Terminal, take a ferry to Toronto Island Park and walk to the lighthouse on the south-west corner of the island | Hours Seasonal based on ferry schedule. See website for more details. | Tip To explore what a Fort York soldier may have looked like, walk down an alley in Dovercourt Village to Capsule Music Store. This music store used to be located closer to Fort York but when it moved, the owners made sure to bring the wooden soldier mannequins with them (985 Dovercourt Road, Toronto, ON M6H 2X6, www.capsulemusic.com).

48_ Gladstone Hotel
Get into bed with art

We all have experienced the drab, standard hotel room, replete with safe pastel and pastoral prints on the walls. The Gladstone Hotel is anything but that.

A travel-weary tourist flips the light switch, and a whole new interpretation of what a hotel room can be flashes in front of their eyes. As Diane von Furstenberg says, "When you get into a hotel room, you lock the door, and you know there is a secrecy, there is a luxury, there is fantasy." Each guest room in the Gladstone has been designed by new and established local artists and designers to create a fantasy that is truly original and immersive. Here, art is an experience that provokes and evokes all ranges of emotion. And as opposed to going to a gallery and viewing art momentarily and moving on, this art installation becomes your bedfellow.

Every January, the Gladstone Hotel hosts a weeklong event called, 'Come Up to My Room'. This provocatively named art festival attracts 4,000 attendees who wander through the alcoves, foyers, hallways, stairwells, Melody Bar, ballroom and eight hotel rooms. For example, in 2014, artist Bruno Billio's work in Room 209, called *Reflections from the Bottom Up*, invited attendees to enter a place of wonder when presented with a fully-mirrored floor and mirrored furniture undersides. The infinite reflection created multiple and endless dimensions to an otherwise square hotel room.

The expressions of art drift down through the stairs and imbue the bottom floors of the hotel with all sorts of exhibitions and music events. You will find the Ryerson Artspace, a unique satellite hub for young, emerging film and photography students to bring their work to a broader audience. The Gladstone Hotel, along with such hotels as the Drake Hotel and the Broadview Hotel, have breathed life into these grand Victorian buildings that line Toronto's historic Queen Street.

Address 1214 Queen Street West, Toronto, ON M6J 1J6, +1 (416) 531-4635, www.gladstonehotel.com, reservations@gladstonehotel.com | Getting there 501 Queen streetcar west to Gladstone Avenue | Hours See website for 'Happenings' schedule | Tip The newly opened Museum of Contemporary Art in the Junction area will provide you another immersive opportunity to explore the creative expressions of contemporary artists (158 Sterling Road, Toronto, ON M6R 2B2, www.moca.ca).

49 — Glenn Gould by the CBC
Visionary musician and complex studio recluse

Like a bronze anchor, the statue of Glenn Gould sits at the base of the Canadian Broadcasting Corporate building, close to Toronto's lakeshore. The statue is installed just outside the Glenn Gould Studio, a broadcasting theatre for Canadian and international performances and recordings. It's aptly placed, since from 1955 to 1964, most of Gould's time was dedicated to studio recordings. Eventually shunning public performances and sheltered from the outside world, Gould embraced what he once called his 'love affair with the microphone.' Indeed, Gould foresaw that studio recording could produce a full tapestry of sound, as opposed to a concert hall, inspiring others such as Alan Parsons, who produced *The Dark Side of the Moon*.

At once a sculpture and a seat, the statue looks like an inquisitive and kind Canadian, bundled up in winter wear, on one side of a park bench. Gazing at the passersby, he seems to beckon and say, 'You can sit with me, and I'll tell you a story.'

And what is this story? Although Gould was recognized internationally as an exceptional pianist and genius, the private man was a complex recluse. The real Gould, a hermit-like introvert, would probably not share a park bench with a stranger. He disliked human touch and was a relentless hypochondriac. Afraid of catching a cold, he wore a winter coat, hat and gloves throughout all seasons. Gould's peculiar behaviour also involved using a low folding chair during concerts that caused him to assume a hunched posture. And he hummed throughout his performances.

Eccentricities aside, Gould's extraordinary recordings of Bach's *Goldberg Variations* have stood the test of time and achieved global legendary status. As journalist Rex Murphy wrote, "He played Bach as saints used to pray: totally immersed, lost in his music." Sit beside him on his eternal bench and ponder his life and contributions to the music world.

Address 250 Front Street West, Toronto, ON M5V 2W6, +1 (416)205-5000, www.cbc.ca/glenngouldstudio, ggsinfo@glenngouldstudio.com | **Getting there** Subway to Union (Line 1); 510 Spadina streetcar to Front Street West | **Hours** Unrestricted | **Tip** From one Canadian icon to another, saunter slightly south and explore the colourful interior of Wayne Gretzky's Toronto, a restaurant and sports bar. Filled with all sorts of hockey memorabilia, the bar takes you back to all the magic moments of Number 99 (99 Blue Jays Way, Toronto, ON M5V9G9, www.gretzkys.com).

50 Good For Her

Celebrating female sexuality one toy at a time

Good For Her is really good for her, him, and anyone who is in touch with their sexuality or trying to discover it. This adult shop is a gold-star example of what a grown-up, sex-positive store should be. There's none of that mainstream, big-boobed, stereotypical porn fare.

Rather, this converted brick house is tastefully decorated with a colourful and charming mural painted on the side of the house, depicting flowers, birds and other images of fertile goddesses. The quaint and friendly exterior invites clientele to leave their trepidations at the door. Once you step inside, the professional and articulate staff makes you feel comfortable right away, so that you can explore and enjoy the experience of shopping for sex toys.

Owner Carlyle Jansen says, 'If you want to learn the techniques and skill of having sex, your doctor isn't going to be the one to teach you.' That's where Good For Her comes in, with its hand-picked sex aids, adult toys and educational and erotic books and DVDs. If that's not enough, there are workshops offered several times a week on various topics such as 'Erotic Massage for Couples', 'The Reluctant Dominatrix', or 'Flirtation A to Z'. These workshops are open to everyone, from those who have just finished chemotherapy, or discovering their latent bisexuality, or long-term married couples who want to reignite their passions – Carlyle Jansen has worked with them all. The workshops are held upstairs from the store and have been running for over a decade. Good For Her contributes to the community as well, most notably running an annual Feminist Porn Film Festival every April, touted as 'mild to wild, straight to queer, smart sexy films for everyone.'

Although the store's focus is celebrating female sexuality, it certainly caters to men and transgender people as well. Variety is the spice of life in this cheery sex-ed emporium.

Address 175 Harbord Street, Toronto, ON M5S 1H3, +1 (416)588-0900, www.goodforher.com | Getting there 510 Spadina streetcar to Harbord Street; 511 Bathurst bus to Harbord Street | Hours Mon–Sat 11am–7pm, Sun 2–6pm | Tip Bampot Bohemian House of Tea and Boardgames (201 Harbord Street, Toronto, ON M5S 1H6, www.bampottea.com) is in a converted house in Harbord Village. Find a cozy corner, order a pot of tea and vegetarian food. Choose from 130 board games and enjoy performances by artists, musicians and spoken word nights for poets.

51 Great China Herbs Centre

Enter an alternative reality and improve your digestion

Adjacent to Toronto's financial core there exists an alternate reality: Toronto's original Chinatown. Brimming with interesting shops, smells and restaurants, this cultural centre is just a few city blocks to the west. Although each storefront is full of intrigue and wonder, there is one store with a rich history that offers an alternative approach to overall human wellness.

Walking past the flurry of vegetable stands and electronic stores, you will find the Great China Herbs Centre. Upon entering, you are quickly greeted by a joyful face and warm tea – "Fabulous for digestion and energy!" you are told. The store is overflowing yet carefully organized. The walls are lined with jars full of herbs and tinctures, all carefully decorated with colourful Chinese labels.

Started by John Chiu in 1967, the Great China Herbs Centre was Toronto's first herbal retailer focusing on Traditional Chinese Medicine (TCM). John's niece, Kim Lamb, took over the shop in 2010. Kim is a compassionate and thoughtful woman with a deep understanding of TCM practices. Full of stories of healing and transformation, her presence is calming and reassuring. Sipping on your tea, you learn about the positive properties of herbs. You come to understand that one herb can have many wide-ranging benefits. Sample some Astragalus Tea and combat the common cold while also preventing infections and aiding digestion. You can ask for a particular remedy, or you can have an assessment from a TCM-trained practitioner who will most certainly prescribe a tea or tincture – for a mere 10 dollars.

Checking out with your herbal purchases, you watch in wonder as the staff tallies up your total with an abacus. You are transported back in time to a period when Confucius guided the minds of many. You feel grounded in the holistic mind, body and soul approach to life and health.

Address 401 Dundas Street West, Toronto, ON M5T 1G6, +1 (416)977-0980, www.greatchinaherbscentre.com | **Getting there** Light Rail Spadina Avenue to Dundas Street; subway to St. Patrick (Line 1), then walk west along Dundas Street | **Hours** Daily 9:30am–6:30pm | **Tip** On the west side of Spadina is the Tap Phong Trading Company. With a wide selection of kitchen utensils, equipment and gadgets and prices less than IKEA, it is sure to satisfy any home cook or aspiring chef (360 Spadina Avenue, Toronto, ON M5T 2G4, www.tapphong.com).

52 The Guild Park and Gardens

Graveyard for Toronto's lost architecture

There are no tombstones here. There are, however, sculptures and exquisite fragments from Toronto's demolished buildings over the past century. The Guild Park and Gardens were brought to life by the creative vision of the Guild Inn's owners, Spencer and Rosa Clark, who purchased the historic inn in 1932. Living atop the Scarborough Bluffs with vast tracks of parkland and forest, the couple built an artist colony and decorated the grounds with pedestals, friezes and facades, all of which escaped the wrecking balls of urban progress. The Clarks saw the art within the architecture in early 20th-century downtown Toronto and made it their mission, at great cost, to preserve these colossal remnants.

The most majestic and ornate of all is the salvaged facade of the old Bank of Toronto, built with classical opulence in 1913. Over time, this white marble assembly of Corinthian columns and sculptured archways and steps has become Toronto's version of the open-air Greek Theatre. Aside from being an outdoor classical theatre venue, it has become a favourite with brides and grooms, history buffs and ever-present urban explorers taking selfies.

As you wander through the vast grounds, you will see ancient, artistic stone relics representing some of Toronto's founding institutions like the Toronto Star Newspaper Building and the Granite Club, each boasting the finest of sculptural stonework of the era. The Clarks amassed more than 60 structures altogether, including some surprises. Being great art connoisseurs, they punctuated the old with modern expressions of Canadian sculpture.

Climb the steps of the Greek Theatre and look out at this surreal graveyard. Your experience will be both edifying and unsettling, as you realize how fleeting the stone markings of civilizations actually are.

Address 201 Guildwood Parkway, Scarborough, ON M1E 1P5, +1 (416)392-8188, www.guildpark.wildapricot.org, friends@guildpark.ca | Getting there Subway to Union (Line 1), then take the GO train to Eglinton GO Station (LE), board 116 Morningside East bus to Guildwood Parkway at Guild Inn East, and walk towards Guildwood Park | Hours See website for seasonal information on visiting and events | Tip If open-air theatre is your passion, go to Shakespeare In High Park, which runs from June to September. Bring a picnic and a comfy lawn chair (1873 Bloor Street West, Toronto, ON M6R 2Z3, www.canadianstage.com).

53 Half House on St Patrick

An optical illusion created by history

Like a setting for a Roald Dahl story, the Half House rests like a visual anomaly on a quiet and unassuming urban pass between Toronto's two major arteries of Queen and Dundas Streets. It attempts to blend into the unassuming streetscape, but it does not succeed. When you turn your head and take a look at this cut-off structure, it's just so stark and strange, like an optical illusion, among the traditional houses and newer buildings that surround it. What happened to the other half?

Built between 1890 and 1893, the Victorian-era bay and gable house originally was part of six identical, structurally intertwined homes on what was known as Drummer Street. During that time, the house was situated in a squalid slum. Old photos show terse and dirty faces, crumbling wall facades and garbage strewn about. Each of the five structures has been taken down with precision, as owners caved into the aggressive tactics of land developers of the mid-20th century. But not 54½ St Patrick Street, which is actually a complete dwelling. For a long time, the house sat empty. A media company bought it and in turn sold it to a group of lawyers who are renovating it extensively.

Curiously, it would be natural to think that the numbering system of 54½ came from its sliced-off existence. In fact, this system existed long before the Half House lost its other half, according to a 1913 insurance policy. This document showed the house shared its numerical particularities with 52½ St Patrick Street as well.

Presently, its neighbours are a major housing development to one side and newer row housing to the other. The new owners are doing a careful renovation of the structure to ensure that it is safe and sound. When the work is done, we can be assured that the Half House will be around for many decades to come and will continue to turn heads and tell its unusual story.

Address 54 ½ St Patrick Street, Toronto, ON M5T 1V1 | Getting there Subway to Osgoode (Line 1); 142 Downtown/Avenue Road Express bus to University Avenue at Queen Street West; 501 Queen streetcar to Simcoe Street West | Hours Unrestricted from the outside only | Tip To find out how to construct a building the correct way, go and check out the University of Toronto's new Daniels Faculty of Architecture building. Check the schedule for public events (230 College Street, Toronto, ON M5T 1R2, www.daniels.utoronto.ca).

54 Hanlan's Beach

York's bare-skinned shoreline

To many, the thought of Toronto having its own bare-skinned shore-line is quite unthinkable. Toronto, or the historic town of York, is, after all a British colony – a city known for its prudish tendencies. However, Hanlan's Beach, Toronto's only nude beach, is perhaps a salute to Canada's British roots after all. When the first British immigrants arrived, swimming au naturel was the preferred norm with numerous clothing optional beaches in Toronto.

Exiting Toronto Island's Hanlan Point Ferry, you are greeted by a life-sized statue of world-champion rower Ned Hanlan, displaying his muscular glory. Hanlan was among the first year-round inhabitants of Toronto Island. He opened the popular Hanlan Hotel adjacent to the beach in the late 1860s, providing an idyllic escape for the city's residents. Following the Great Depression, bathing suit rules shifted worldwide, and Hanlan's Point languished. Over time, though, the gay community embraced the beach, and finally in 1999, the City of Toronto allowed Hanlan's Point to return to its bare-skinned roots.

It is a short walk or bike ride from the ferry to the beach. Wander through the driftwood gate and down the beach path. What awaits you, secluded behind sand dunes and brush, is one of Toronto's finest beaches. Troubles melt away while enjoying the laid-back vibe, aqua blue waters and picturesque western cityscapes. With clear signage delineating the one-km-long beach into clothing or clothing optional areas, there is no beach anarchy. There are mixtures of young and old, families and singles, gays and straights. Dipping your toes into the notoriously cold water, you will be comforted by the sandy bottom. Although the beach season is short, make sure not to miss this most secluded part of Toronto Island, free from society's conventions. Come enjoy the lake breeze and frolic naked in the summer sun.

Address Lakeshore Avenue, Toronto, ON M5J 2W2, +1 (416)293-8196, www.torontoisland.com/hanlans.php | Getting there Ferry from Jack Leyton Ferry Terminal (9 Queens Quay West, Toronto, ON M5J 2H3) | Hours Unrestricted | Tip Hanlan's Point was once home to a baseball stadium. Interestingly it is where Babe Ruth hit his first professional home run in 1914. Look for the plaque as you exit the ferry, adjacent to Ned Hanlan's statue.

55_Henderson Brewing Company

Every bottle of beer tells a Toronto story

Steve Himel, co-founder of Henderson Brewing Company, wants to bring the community together over a bottle of consistently excellent beer. Not your highbrow variety mind you, but rather a refreshing and flavourful beer to quaff with your chums. Located in Toronto's lower junction triangle, Henderson's intends to be more than just an off-sales establishment. It aims to be a destination and a community hub, where all can mix and mingle, meet one another and brush off the dust of the day. Mark Benzaquen, Henderson's co-founder and accomplished brewmaster, has created award-winning beers: Henderson's Best and Food Truck. These are the company's flagship decoctions, available at both the beer and liquor stores.

To really understand the brand, you need to go to where the owners' imagination is on full display. Ideally situated beside the West Rail Trail, the brewery seeks out the stories behind some of Toronto's fascinating people and places and interprets these with beer products. The name Henderson is an homage to the city's first genuine brewmaster, Robert Henderson. Every mid-month Henderson launches the limited run of a new beer, customizing the flavours and the labels, to resonate with a tale yet to be told, a bit of Toronto's history in need of celebration. These brews can only be sampled and procured on site.

At every monthly event, you will be treated to the backstory behind the beer by storyteller Himel himself, and be the first to savour that month's new flavour. If you are lucky and the subject of the storyline is still alive and willing, you could have your sample signed by the person of the moment, making your bottled brew a collector's item.

Events at Henderson's include food pop-ups, poetry readings, 'vinyl show & tells,' and many others. The brewery tours are a must do.

Address 128 Sterling Road, Toronto, ON M6P 0A1, +1 (416)863-8822,
www.hendersonbrewing.com | **Getting there** Subway to Dundas West (Line 2);
506 Carlton streetcar to Dundas Street | **Hours** Daily 11am–10pm | **Tip** If you're hungry
for a meal, walk right next door to The Drake Commissary. An outpost of the Drake
Hotel, it is a bakery, bar, and larder (128 Sterling Road, Toronto, ON M6P 0A1,
www.drakecommissary.ca).

56 Henley's Hideaway

Welcome to the tiny home of an adventurous hedgehog

Along the tree strewn path at Kew Gardens park south of Queen Street in the Toronto Beaches neighbourhood, near the beautiful plantings and the library, is Henley the Hedgehog's Hideaway. You can't miss Henley's fairy home, with its front door at the base of a tree just beyond several stately oaks.

Henley the Hedgehog is the creation of a grade school teacher and self-published author, Sharon Douris. Douris uses Henley and his fictional exploits as a way to make reading and the classroom come alive. The Beaches native was searching for a pet of her own but suffered from the itching and sneezing often associated with allergic reactions to traditional pets. After analyzing the range of hypoallergenic possibilities, she fell on the idea of adopting a hedgehog. Thus, Henley, the adorable pet and the fictional character, entered her life and inspired the pages of her books.

Now starring in a three-book series, Henley, named after the British town of Henley-on-Thames, has his own Instagram and Facebook accounts, where the handsome hedgehog can be seen sipping Pippins tea and wearing a sombrero. The books chronicle his many adventures, including the one where he gets his head stuck down a hole, and the everyday dilemmas of searching for a rain barrel. Is Sharon Douris a modern day Beatrix Potter or A. A. Milne?

Arriving at Henley's oak tree, look for the arched door carefully crafted by Douris' husband Nick Robins, with its beautifully antiqued hinges, the front entrance for this small celebrity mammal's home. Originally used as a photo shoot for her books, the magical tree dwelling has quickly become a secret neighbourhood play area for local kids. Decorated by the local children (and some adults too), the fairy home features miniature landscaping, chairs and figurines. Notes are often written and left for Henley, and some people even use his home as a wishing well.

Address 2075 Queen Street East, Toronto, ON M4E 2N9, +1 (416)392-2489, www.instagram.com/henley_the_hedgehog | Getting there 143 Downtown/Beach Express bus to Lee Avenue at Queen Street East; 64 Main bus to Hambly Avenue at Queen Street East; 501 Queen streetcar to Lee Avenue | Hours Unrestricted | Tip Wander along Queen Street East, visiting the outstanding independent retailers and restaurants of the Beaches neighbourhood (www.torontolife.com/tag/queen-street-east).

57__High Park Club
Come slide some stones

In Toronto's west end is High Park, Toronto's largest park, complete with winding hiking trails, a zoo, sports facilities and a plethora of playgrounds. Hidden just east of this beautiful green space, in the neighbourhood of Roncesvalles, is the park's hidden jewel, the High Park Club. This historic, red-brick building is home to the oldest curling club in Canada and the first of its kind in Toronto. Constructed well over 100 years ago, this landmark was originally established when this part of the city was mostly dirt roads and farmland.

Entering through the rather dark rear of the building, you would hardly describe the curling fraternity entrance as chic or welcoming. However, you are quickly surrounded with the sporting spirit of times past. With five sheets of ice, the club celebrates the sport of curling and its many participants, from rudimentary beginners to Canadian champions, as witnessed by the well-populated trophy cases and bulletin boards. Invented by the Scots in the 1600s, curling is one of the oldest team sports in the world. Although the sport did not make its way to Canada until the 1800s, it has become an important part of Canada's identity, its international athletic successes and its winter traditions.

Curling has always been known for its democratic tendencies, particularly in the military clubs where people of different ranks have played together. The High Park Club is no different. You are able to borrow their brooms and join mixed, single gender, competitive and social leagues as you slip and slide across the ice. Rent the ice if you dare to create your own *bonspiel*, or curling tournament, and the club will even provide an instructor if needed. Crown your accomplishments or drown your losses with a well-deserved Canadian lager at the fully stocked bar, celebrating a favourite Canadian pastime in this elegant timeless treasure.

Address 100 Indian Road, Toronto, ON M6R 2V4, +1 (416)536-8054, www.highparkclub.com |
Getting there Subway to Keele (Line 2), then take 80 Queensway bus towards Sherway to
Parkside Drive at Garden Avenue; 501 Queen streetcar east to the Queensway at Glendale
Avenue | **Hours** See website for hours and visitor information | **Tip** Consider crossing Park-
side Avenue that runs parallel to Indian Road and visit the west side of the 400-acre High
Park. In the spring, the park hosts the Cherry Blossom Festival. In the summer and fall, the
gardens are irresistible, and in the winter, you can skate on Grenadier Pond (1873 Bloor Street
West, Toronto, ON M6R 2Z3, www.highparktoronto.com).

58 Hot Docs
Ted Rogers Cinema

If these walls could talk

In 1913 when the Madison Theater opened in Toronto, it was one of the first motion picture cinemas in the city. Although the original theater has been demolished and rebuilt, the creative crusading spirit has remained in the form of Hot Docs Cinema. The theatre has oscillated between a popular neighbourhood cinema packed for weekend matinees and horror double features, to a heavily censored adult film theatre – if those walls could talk… The original theatre often played art and cult films, such as the cult-favorite *Rocky Horror Picture Show*. Keeping with tradition, this newer version still screens *Rocky Horror* with a live cast on the last Friday of each month.

By 2010, the Bordonaro family purchased the building, later partnering with Hot Docs Canadian International Documentary Festival, and the Hot Docs Cinema was born, becoming the hub of the world-renowned festival. The theatre is busy year-round as well, as the home for first-run Canadian and international documentaries. In fact, with seating for 710 viewers, it is the largest theatre in the world exclusively focused on the important art form of documentary filmmaking. There is a carefully curated movie selection for the educated, curious and diverse clientele.

Upon entering the renovated cinema, you'll appreciate that the architects have embraced technical advances while leaving historical charm, perfect for an awesome cinematic adventure. Grabbing your popcorn, and yes that is *real butter*, you are unexpectedly taken by the fabulous craft beer and wine selection. Balancing a glass of your favourite pinot gris, you join the other theatregoers. Perhaps venture up to the balcony where the cinema's original wider and more comfortable 'love seats' reside. This cushy nest will be perfect for you and a friend to enjoy a night out with wine, snacks, and a world-class documentary.

Address 506 Bloor Street West, Toronto, ON M5S 1Y3, +1 (416)637-3123, www.hotdocscinema.ca, boxoffice@hotdocs.ca | Getting there Subway to Bathurst (Line 2) | Hours See website for showtimes | Tip The Mount Pleasant Theatre is one of Toronto's oldest surviving cinemas. It offers original, thought-provoking movies and remains an integral part of the film community (675 Mount Pleasant Road, Toronto, ON M4S 2N2, www.cinemaclock.com/ont/toronto/theatres/mount-pleasant).

59 — The Hole in the Wall

This wedged-in bar is no hole in the wall

Recessed between two neighbouring shops, the Hole in the Wall Bar provides a narrow escape from the streets, and a welcoming respite from Toronto's workaday world. The original building, built in 1900, has housed a café, a toy store, and a dress shop to name a few. The type of commercial establishments have changed throughout the years, but not the name; it's always been 'The Hole in the Wall'. The quirky layout of the space is what makes this a destination for anyone looking for a cozy venue for comfort food, live music, craft beer and an astounding collection of whiskies.

The place has the ergonomics of a submarine, long and narrow, although it looks nothing like the inside of a submarine. Exposed red brick, oversized vintage chandeliers, dark wood and the welcoming reflection of bottles from the massive bar, make this neighbourhood gem feel like a cover for a book on *hygge*. What is hygge? Voted word of the year in 2016, this Danish, and now universal word, means a combination of coziness, charm, comfort and kinship. And you can find it in dollops at the Hole in the Wall, a place that is no more than 10-feet wide, but always seems to have a place just for you.

The owners, brothers Ben and Jack Wilkinson, have developed a local menu with a Latin American twist, including local trout and organic fare. Live music graces the establishment most nights, with the musicians and serving staff practicing a well-choreographed ballet of controlled coordination in the back area of the bar. The brothers know their musicians, since they also run another live music venue in the Junction area called the Junction City Music Hall, a place described by Toronto bloggers as being 'where you're part of a secret club that only cool kids know about.'

The Hole in the Wall, with its tongue-in-cheek moniker, is truly no hole in the wall, and delivers a fun, welcoming atmosphere for its clients every day of the week.

Address 2867 Dundas Street West, Toronto, ON M6P 1Y9, +1 (647)350-3564, www.theholeinthewallto.ca, theholeinthewallto@gmail.com | **Getting there** Subway to Keele (Line 2), then 89 Weston North bus to Dundas Street West; by car, from midtown, drive west on Dupont Street, after the underpass merge onto Dundas Street West | **Hours** Mon–Sat 4pm–2am, Sun 11–2am | **Tip** A couple of doors down, check out the Rod and Gun Barbershop. Taxidermy, beer and outdoor Canadiana are found between mirrors and razors, a true original (2877 Dundas Street West, Toronto, ON M6P 1Y9, www.rodgunandbarbers.com).

60 Hugh's Room Live

As Joni Mitchell says 'Songs are like tattoos.'

Hugh's Room Live is not really a room, but a testament of what can happen when the whole experience is bigger than the sum of its parts. What does this mean? Hugh's Room closed in early 2017 because of financial difficulties and could have been a memory in Toronto, like other former live music venues. But something happened that sparked the will and imagination of music lovers to band together and revive the venue. Revive it they did, and arguably more than that. They collected $150,000 from 500 supporters, implemented a new financial model and hired a chef and powerhouse music curator to book the programming. The line up of musicians it is now attracting, coupled with the fresh excitement around the place, will guarantee it will be around for the foreseeable future.

Hugh's Room has now become Hugh's Room Live, and the venue has been voted one of the best places in the city for live music by many high-profile musicians. There is no such thing as a bad seat in this downward-tiered venue space with the stage at the bottom. It's an opportunity to have an adult night out, with an impressive a la carte menu to order dinner from and enjoy before the performance. A well-fed audience is an attentive one.

The magic of Hugh's Room Live begins when the first note reverberates in the space. It could be folk, the musical heritage of the venue, blues or rock. There are also theme evenings and music festivals, attracting groups of musicians with their bands. Derek Andrews, a music curator who has assembled major music festivals across the country, will make sure that you will be musically transported. In this era of disappearing independent live music venues, Hugh's Room Live is a testament to Toronto's commitment to carrying on the live music scene. A destination on burgeoning Roncesvalles Avenue, Hugh's Room Live is hitting a new note in live music in Toronto.

Address 2261 Dundas Street West, Toronto, ON M6R 1X6, +1 (416)533-5483, www.hughsroomlive.com, info@hughsroomlive.com | Getting there Subway to Dundas West (Line 2) | Hours Box office daily noon–7pm, doors open at 6pm | Tip For a more Latin and World Music take on the dinner and live music experience in the city, get your salsa shoes shined up and head over to the loud and proud Lula Lounge (1585 Dundas Street West, Toronto, ON M6K 1T9, www.lula.ca).

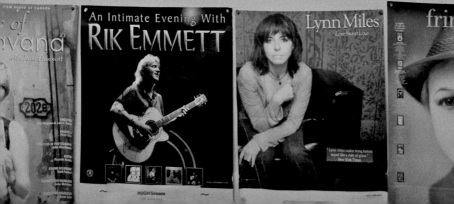

61 Humber Bay Arch Bridge
Bridging the past and the present

Located in a somewhat unsightly stretch of Lake Ontario's shoreline, west of the downtown core, one comes upon an important landmark. Surrounded by green space and apartment buildings, the Humber Bay Arch Bridge is an elegantly designed, dove-white arch bridge at the mouth of the Humber River, an ancient aboriginal trading route. The bridge is not only a welcome addition to present-day Toronto, but also a salute to the city's past. The Humber, a Canadian Heritage River, was one of the first natural landmarks routing First Nations people to Georgian Bay and Lake Simcoe in the north. Today, the bridge represents a beautiful anchor point for the Martin Goodman pedestrian, recreation and cyclist trail while carefully protecting the environmental balance of the Humber River.

This world-renowned engineering feat was collaboratively constructed in the mid-1900s, for a price tag slightly over $4 million. The designers of the bridge came from many disciplines, including a celebrated First Nations' art consultant and the Montgomery Sisam Architects of Toronto. Constructed from two high-strength steel pipes bent into two arches, the deck is suspended by 40 plus stainless-steel hangers.

Walking across the 100-meter bridge, look up and view the Thunderbird, an important symbol to First Nations people, representing the Seer of All. Explore the pathway underneath the bridge where turtles, snakes, salmon and canoes are displayed, again commemorating the First Nations influence on the bridge, as well as the former natural inhabitants of the area. With a brilliant backdrop of the Toronto skyline in the distance, the area becomes romantic and breathtaking in the evenings. Whether you come to explore the bridge and its splendor or use it as a launch point for further trail adventures, the bridge and its glory represent an important element of Toronto's thoughtful imagination.

Address South of Lake Shore Boulevard West, Martin Goodman Trail, Toronto, ON |
Getting there Cycle or walk south of Lake Shore Boulevard following the Martin Goodman
Trail west; subway to Keele (Line 2) and board the West bus 80 toward Sherway to Ellis at
Lake Shore Boulevard West | Hours Unrestricted | Tip Explore the many trails and parks
along Lake Ontario and the Humber River. The adjacent Humber Bay Park West is
beautiful anytime of year and a great place to view the Toronto skyline (Legion Road &
Lake Shore Boulevard West, Etobicoke, ON, www.toronto.ca).

62 Inkdigenous Tattoo
Body art delineates roots

Gone are the days when suitcases were plastered with sticker souvenirs displaying travel destinations. Now, the body is the canvas. Sure, a simple Canadian maple leaf might do, but why not delve deeper into our nation's cultural history?

Iroquois warriors would tally up vanquished foes with tattoo designs. Cree used them for religious rituals and Inuit women enhanced their beauty with facial markings. Sharp animal bones were used to puncture skin before rubbing coal and okra into the wounds.

Inkdigenous Tattoo has made everything a whole lot easier with their state-of-the-art equipment. All of the artists are First Nations members, and they specialize in cultural motifs, both old and new. The owner, Toby Sicks, gives background info about each design. The eagle, he explains, is the messenger to our Creator; the feather reminds us of our spiritual connection to the Divine. Aside from clan designs and woodland art, this tattoo parlour also offers healing symbols created to soothe and restore body, mind and spirit. In fact, a shell smudging bowl, sage and sweetgrass greet the client at the front entrance.

Above all, Inkdigenous Tatoo provides an educational experience. Akin to a small, intimate art museum, the walls are lined with original paintings and prints by local Indigenous artists. Beaded jewelry, handmade leather pouches and T-shirts with aboriginal designs are also for sale. Sicks has provided a studio space endorsing the talents of his cultural community. He is passionate about sharing his knowledge about the sweat lodge, dream catchers and our connection to Mother Earth. And as a former social worker, Sicks donates part of the proceeds back into the community to further support and develop Indigenous language and culture.

Here you can get an original tattoo, buy amazing art or, at the very least, leave knowing so much more about our country's roots.

Address 124 Jarvis Street, Toronto, ON M5B 2B5, +1 (647)575-8629, www.inkdigenoustattoo.com, inkdigenoustattoos@gmail.com | Getting there 501 Queer streetcar to Jarvis Street; 141 Downtown/Mt Pleasant Express bus to Queen Street | Hc Daily 10am–8pm | Tip If you want some ideas for tattoos, go to the Daphne Cockwell Gallery of Canada: First Peoples at the Royal Ontario Museum for inspiration on Indiger iconography (100 Queen's Park, Toronto, ON M5S 2C6, www.rom.on.ca).

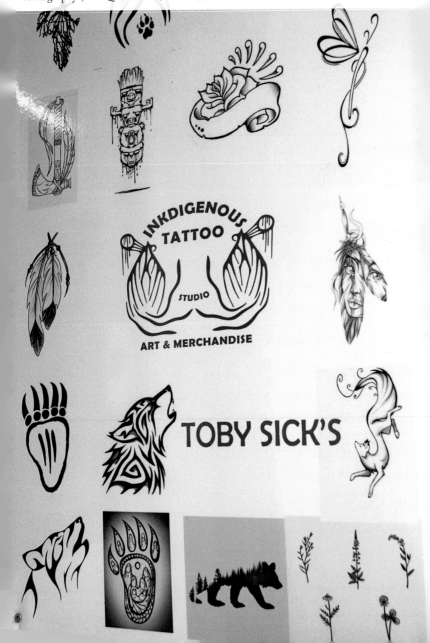

63 Inukshuk Park
Giant stone guide

Towering over the Lake Ontario shoreline is a stone sculpture waiting to embrace and guide us. This giant inuksuk, with its human-like qualities and outstretched arms, looks both inviting and quite impressive. ('Inukshuk' is the Anglicized version of the Inuktitut term, 'inuksuk'.)

On the Martin Goodman Trail, a small stone staircase leads to one of the largest inuksuks in North America, standing 9 metres, or 30 feet, high with an arm span of 4.5 metres, or 15 feet. Peering through the stone structure, you'll see the calm waters of Lake Ontario, a quaint marina and a beautiful skyscape.

In the Inuit language, *inuksuk* means 'in the likeness of a human', and guides travellers while providing comfort, advice and spatial orientation, which is especially crucial in the tundra. This particular inuksuk is a powerful symbol for visitors to the lake and the Lakeshore drivers. Although these unworked stone sculptures are typically built and used by aboriginal groups and are most often found in the Arctic landscape, it is creatively appropriate that Toronto now has its own stone guide. It was built for the official launch of World Youth Day 2002 and the visit of Pope John Paul II to Toronto, reminding us that, like each inuksuk stone, we are each a separate entity, but our strength lies in our unity.

The Toronto Inukshuk is the creative work of Kellypalik Qimirpik, an internationally renowned Inuit artist from Cape Dorset, Nunavut, who passed away in 2017. Qimirpik consulted for the City on the project and assisted with all aspects of the project from the initial sculpture design to the selection of the rose granite used to create the cairn. Kellypalik carefully carved the individual pieces from 50 tons of stone while heavy machinery put them into place. The result: a tribute to Native Canadians elegantly reminding us of the inuksuk's unifying power.

Address 789 Lake Shore Boulevard West, Toronto, ON M5V 3T7, +1 (416)338-4386, www.toronto.ca | Getting there Subway to Union (Line 1), then take 509 Harbour-front East bus to Manitoba Drive at Strachan Avenue; walk or cycle directly via the Martin Goodman Trail | Hours Daily 8am–11pm | Tip Cross Lakeshore Boulevard and be blessed by the angel at The Princes' Gates to the Canadian National Exposition (CNE). She holds up high a single maple leaf over this triumphal arch that was built to commemorate 60 years of Canadian confederation (11 Princes' Boulevard, Toronto, ON M6K 3C3, www.theex.com).

64 Ireland Park

Remembering the coffin ships

Toronto's history is filled with the shifting tides of immigrants, perhaps most notably in the summer of 1847, when thousands of Irish immigrants landed on the shores of Muddy York, as Toronto has been called. Over 38,000 Irish arrived with empty pockets and empty stomachs on the banks of this great city in order to flee Irish famine. Although Toronto had only 20,000 inhabitants at the time, the Irish newcomers dropped anchor with the great hope for a new life in a new land. Thousands who arrived in the bleak 'coffin ships' from Ireland did not survive the crossing, and many perished from 'ship fever,' or typhus, in fever sheds erected on the shores of Lake Ontario.

Ireland Park, which was opened in the summer of 2007, is dedicated to the 1,185 Irish men, women and children who departed from an assortment of Irish ports and perished during the crossing. Full of symbolism, it is a place of contemplation and reflection. Ireland Park has a sister park in Dublin. The Dublin Park symbolizes departure with seven bronze statues, while only five beaten souls are represented at the arrival or Toronto Park.

This important landmark is located adjacent to Toronto City Airport on Eireann or Irish Quay. The life-size realistic bronzed statues as you enter the park are indeed disturbing. There is a malnourished and sickly commonality to all of the figures. A hungry, pregnant woman, gripping her child, looks to be clinging to life itself. An orphaned boy is pensively looking back, while a woman lies sprawled across the cold earth. Behind these haggard souls, who gleam out over the modern day Toronto skyline, is a grand block of Irish limestone shaped to resemble a ship. Examine it closely as the names of Atlantic voyage victims are engraved between the chunks of stone. The park is an important and poignant memorial, honouring a transformative event in Toronto's history.

Address Queens Quay West, Toronto, ON M5V 3G3, +1 (416)601-6906, irelandparkfoundation.com, admin@irelandparkfoundation.com | Getting there From Bathurst Street & Queens Quay, walk south to the foot of the boardwalk on the waterfront | Hours Daily 8am–11pm | Tip To celebrate another important Toronto community, stop by Norway Park (659 Queens Quay West, Toronto, ON M5V 3N2, www.toronto.ca). The 2.4-hectare, or 6-acre park features a ball diamond, a children's playground and many paths throughout the gardens. Its name commemorates the World War II training base used by the Norwegian Air Force that once existed at this site.

65 __ Knife

The samurai experience for modern-day chefs

Famous photographer Diane Arbus once wrote, 'The world can only be grasped by action, not by contemplation. The hand is the cutting edge of the mind.' Eugene Ong, owner of Knife, would add to that and say that the knife is the cutting edge of the hand. His passion is knives – not the ones that hang on walls like trophies or museum pieces, but ones that are used several times daily.

Starting his career as a chef, he would sit and cut 10 bags of onions at a time, which gave him plenty of time to contemplate the beauty and importance of knives. After decades of high-end professional cooking and world travelling, Eugene settled down in Toronto and launched his retail business, Knife, in a small Queen Street West store. Fast forward many years, and Knife opened its biggest and boldest retail outlet yet in late 2017. The new location allows Eugene to not only sell knives and other chef-inspired implements, but also to offer knife care and use classes. The space is long and organic, yet cool looking, playing on the aesthetics of a handmade knife.

Most of the traditions and meticulous skills surrounding the making of Japanese knives started back in the day of the samurai warriors. Since head chopping is not as common as lettuce head cutting, the swords have now transformed into kitchen knives. Yet the same care in the making of these knives is apparent; high-quality metals forged with masters banging their skillful hammers to create the ultimate kitchen tool. Chefs comprise the largest clientele at Knife, but foodies and culinary aficionados do frequent the store as well.

Apart from knives, Knife sells Japanese barbeques, locally sourced cutting boards and other kitchen tools. It also offers knife-sharpening services that are extremely popular with Toronto chefs. You will never have a dull moment at Knife, since the shop will always make sure you have a cutting edge.

Address 803 Dundas Street West, Toronto, ON M6J 1V2, +1 (647)996-8609, www.knifetoronto.com | Getting there 505 Dundas streetcar to Dundas Street West & Bathurst Street | Hours Mon & Tue 11am–7pm, Wed–Sat 11am–6pm, Sun noon–5pm | Tip Where would Drake launch his flagship store OVO in Toronto? Well, Dundas West of course (899 Dundas Street West, Toronto, ON M6J 1W1, us.octobersveryown.com). So much fashion-forward retailing is available on this strip, it's hard to name just one. How about Canadian cutting edge fashion pioneer, Comrags? (812 Dundas Street West, Toronto, ON M6J 1V3, www.comrags.com).

66 Koerner Hall Atrium

Turns out that a chitarrone is not a type of pasta

Have you ever heard of a *pochette* or a *chitarrone*? Or how about a *flageolet*, a member of the fipple flute family? If you think this is a tongue-twister, you are on the right wavelength because all of these objects have to do with making music. Welcome to the Koerner Hall Atrium.

Go through the Victorian stone gates and follow the path of the Philosopher's Walk that leads you to the stairs of the Atrium. The b Espresso Bar, wedged in an atrium between the two radically different eras of buildings, will greet you. Grab an espresso or a latte, and start to wander the halls at the back and over the café on the second floor. You have now discovered the Early Instrument Collection, replete with fretted clavichords and double manual harpsichords, and the one-keyed ebony walking stick flute from the 18th century. Imagine owning one of these flutes – you could hike and play a tune any time the inspiration strikes.

Michael and Sonja Koerner have been active in arts philanthropy for over 40 years after amassing a fortune in the energy sector of Canada. This influential couple has been on the boards of almost all of the large-scale arts organizations in Canada. Michael's personal passion over decades has been collecting old and rare instruments, as well as art related to music.

After you have explored the musical treasure trove on the first floor, go up the steps to view miniature displays of Chinese pottery depicting 2nd-century BC musicians, or ornate peg boxes for *viola da gambas*. Or lift your gaze to admire the ROM Crystal form clearly seen from the Atrium windows.

This million-dollar collection is yours to view for free, thanks to the donation provided by the Koerners. This unique and fascinating collection is not found on any webpage, but it is known to Royal Conservatory students and concertgoers. And now, to you.

Address 273 Bloor Street West, Toronto, ON M5S 1W2, +1 (416)408-0208, www.tso.ca/venue/koerner-hall | Getting there Subway to St. George (Line 1), or Museum (Line 2) | Hours Mon–Fri 10am–6pm, Sat noon–6pm, Sun & holidays open three hours prior to performance start time | Tip Koerner Hall is one of North America's most beautiful and acoustically superb concert halls. This is where the Royal Conservatory presents classical and world music concerts. Attend a concert and enjoy the unique displays surrounding the concert hall as you enjoy the whole concert experience (273 Bloor Street West, Toronto, ON M5S 1W2, www.rcmusic.com).

67 Lillian H. Smith Library

Early childhood and sci-fi in the special collections

The Lillian Smith Library is both a neighbourhood library and a treasure trove of collections that will delight any bibliophile who wishes to be swept far away. The two collections that command their own floors are the Osborne Early Childhood Collection and the Merrill Collection of Science Fiction, Speculation and Fantasy. Each collection has its own website and sponsors its own book launches, exhibits and interest groups.

The Osborne Collection boasts a collection of over 80,000 rare and modern children's books and 5,000 pieces of original art. It is surrounded by carefully curated exhibits that any book lover would adore. The cherished children's book character and lovable canine rogue, Harry the Dirty Dog, has attained mascot status here at the collection.

Come and get spaced out at the Merrill Collection, which was originally called 'the spaced out collection' by Judith Merrill herself. She was a celebrated science fiction writer who donated her personal collection to the Toronto Public Library in 1970. Since then, it has become the largest publicly accessed science fiction collection in North America. Interested in graphic novels and fantasy role-playing games? Wish to view the original edition of *Dracula*? You have found your literary launchpad. Academic researchers and world-renowned authors travel to Toronto and this facility to find the authoritative texts they need, and it's yours to access free of charge, six days a week.

Walk through the doors of imagination, guarded by a winged griffin and a winged lion at the Lillian Smith Library, and explore the worlds of classical children's tales and fantastical storybook images from the 'what if' genre of science fiction. That way, as Judith Merrill says, you too can participate in 'wonder – informed, thoughtful, purposeful wonder' as you ask the librarian to guide you on your rare-book hunt.

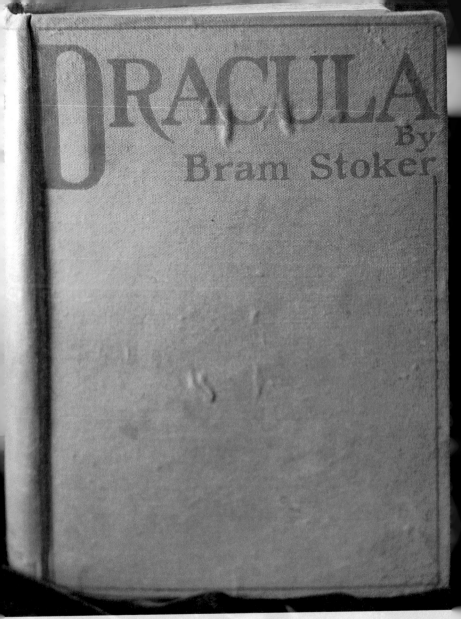

DRACULA
By
Bram Stoker

Address 239 College Street, Toronto, ON M5T 1R5, +1 (416)393-7753,
www.torontopubliclibrary.ca/lillianhsmith, lsstaff@torontopubliclibrary.ca | Getting there
Subway to College Street (Line 1) | Hours Mon–Fri 10am–6pm, Sat 9am–5pm | Tip
Explore the architectural wonder of the Toronto Reference Library, which serves as a beehive
of research activity. Located conveniently in the middle of the city, it is a go-to spot for book
launches, collections, study space and all information in the public library system (789 Yonge
Street, Toronto, ON M4W 2G8, www.torontopubliclibrary.ca/torontoreferencelibrary).

68 __ The Little House

Small property with a big reputation

You might think that the tiny house movement is a modern trend in the last few years. Well, Torontonians were ahead of the curve when the Little House was built in 1912 as a contractor's creative solution when a laneway between two houses was proposed but did not have the support of a Mr. Arthur Weeden. To prevent its construction, Weeden built a 314-square-foot house, which still stands on Day Avenue. This tiny structure, with its picturesque gabled roof and white wood exterior, complete with front patio and a stone walkway, has prompted interest from curiosity seekers and neighbours since it was built over 100 years ago.

Weeden lived there for 25 years with his wife, tending to their small vegetable garden and sleeping in the tiny one bedroom in the back of the house. Since then, the house has changed hands many times, and even hosted new immigrant families with children!

In 2008, when the house was on the market again, Ellen DeGeneres phoned the listing realtor during a segment of her show and discussed how interested she was in the listing. News of this little house and all of its tiny mouse house features was broadcast across North America on *Ellen*, with her detailing its efficient layout as she peppered the listing with her hilarious observations. The real estate agent was thrilled with the coverage as she earnestly answered Ellen's concerns.

Perhaps unknowingly, Ellen's broadcast sparked the imagination of the inspired tiny house movement. In spite of its size, the house has a basement, back and front patios and parking for two cars. Take that condo dwellers! This house has inspired a famous song as well, 'Come Back to Me', by Maria Lee Carta, although it's not easy to lose someone in a 300-square-foot house. This little house has influenced builders, artists, lovers and media celebrities. What would it inspire in you?

Address 128 Day Street, Toronto, ON M6E 3W2 | **Getting there** 29 Dufferin bus to Dufferin at Rogers Road; 161 Rogers bus to Rogers Road at Boon Avenue | **Hours** Unrestricted from the outside only | **Tip** If you are into the tiny worlds, the Little Dollhouse Company is filled with miniature furniture, dishes and many other charming items to furnish a stylish doll's home (612 Mount Pleasant Road, Toronto, ON M4S 2M8, www.thelittledollhousecompany.com).

69 Mackenzie House Press

Toronto's first mayor of the truly rebellious type

Originally from Scotland, William Lyon Mackenzie was the forefather of modern-day Toronto. His values clashed with the appointed elites as he had a strong, heretical view that everyone should be regarded equally on this new soil. He explosively expounded on this view with his weapon of choice, the newspaper. With the aid of his beloved Gutenburg-style printing press, Mackenzie created broadsheets that cried out for locally representative government in the face of British appointed officials. In 1834, Mackenzie's progressive opinions connected with the people, and he became the first mayor of Toronto. It also was the first time that this sprawling urban town on the shores of Lake Ontario was officially called The City of Toronto, and not York. Change was in the air.

After a career replete with rebellion, expulsion and subsequent return, his supporters bought this fiery politician and journalist a handsome home on Bond Street in 1858. This house and present-day museum is a splendid example of middle-class home life in the 1850s. It is where Mackenzie lived the last two years of his life, happily accompanied by his beloved printing press. The large press, which helped form the opinions of Torontonians, travelled with him for decades, and the Mackenzie House was no exception. Set up originally in a structure next to the outdoor privies, it has now been carefully relocated indoors and sits honorably at the entrance to the museum.

The exceptional Mackenzie House tour helps you discover the meaning of 'cut to the chase' and 'coin a phrase'. Perhaps you will express your opinions and create your own newspaper sheet. After carefully setting the movable type, your sheet moves through the printer's press, just as it did in the mid-1850s. William Lyon Mackenzie's progressive ideas moved through this very press and are still around the city today.

Address 82 Bond Street, Toronto, ON M5B 1X2, +1 (416)392-6915, www.toronto.ca/explore-enjoy/history-art-culture/museums/mackenzie-house | **Getting there** Subway to Dundas (Line 1) | **Hours** Sat & Sun noon–5pm | **Tip** Trip Print Press is an organized printing press specializing in fine mercantile printing. Explore the amazingly curated collection of lead and wood producing custom contemporary and traditional letterpress printing and order custom business and social stationary (468 Cumberland Avenue, Unit 1D, Hamilton, ON L8M 3M5, www.tripprintpress.ca).

70 Merchants of Green Coffee

High integrity, great tasting coffee

Tucked away on Matilda Street just north of Queen East is a large, clandestine coffee shop. Merchants of Green Coffee is a business germinated in 1994 by five friends who took it upon themselves to bring coffee integrity to Toronto. As green, fair trade coffee pioneers, pre-dating the arrival of Starbucks and friends, they originally had a sole distribution focus. Their purpose was to have coffee drinkers everywhere understand the 'hows and wheres' of their coffee beans.

Selling originally through restaurants and markets, the owners of Green Coffee did not begin with a café or espresso bar in mind. However, the quality of their message and their coffee combined with the beauty of their space created a welcoming home for the local community.

A former tannery, the pre-war industrial space is as attractive outside as it is inside. The red-brick beauty displays the gentle idealism of the early 90s versus the techno straight lines of today. It is inviting and safe. With a bright red coffee roaster, exposed wood beams and a well-loved upright piano, it has a warm eclecticism. The environment is filled with delicious coffee, and exemplifies the commitment to a 'green focus'. There are used books, recycled furniture and even a repurposed espresso bar. The beautifully bold but not bitter coffee is made from carefully selected beans from far-off places and elegantly served in a wine carafe. With its strong community feel, it has evolved into a place for live music, readings and even weddings. For those who choose to learn more about their beans there is a top-rated coffee school. With sunny south-facing windows, you relax into the vibe and the WiFi. The cheerful staff has a proud coffee knowledge and expertise. If you're a coffee fan, espresso, regular, or even decaf, you will not be disappointed by what many agree is the best java in the city.

Address 2 Matilda Street, Toronto, ON M4M 1L9, +1 (416)741-5369, www.merchantsofgreencoffee.com | **Getting there** 505 Dundas streetcar east to Monroe Street; 503 Kingston Road bus to Queen Street East at Carroll Street | **Hours** Mon–Fri 8am–6pm, Sat & Sun 9am–6pm | **Tip** Check out the nearby Joel Weeks park, with its very funny squirrel sculpture (10 Thompson Street, Toronto, ON M4M 1L9).

71 Mjölk

Coaxing out the art

Mjölk is a 'shop-house' within the pre-war streetscape of the Junction neighborhood. This fiercely proud neighbourhood is identified both by its defined physical boundaries, created by train corridors and true grit, and the proud 'Junctionites' who are the creative stewards of the quickly changing community. Juli and John Baker, artists extraordinaire, developed their Scandinavian/Japanese shop-house with the philosophy to promote a curated lifestyle experience. Mjölk is a combination of re-crafted Scandinavian furniture with Japanese household items where 'everything has a soul.'

When you step into the shop and onto a white stained plywood floor, the faint smell of incense that greets you gives rise to feelings of stillness. Your eyes scan over natural elements of copper, hardwood, plant life, ceramics, wool and opaline glass. You realize that, as John says, "There is beauty to be found in even the simplest everyday tools." Every object in this shop-house has a purpose, thought through by the husband and wife duo, the artist, and maybe even a local artisanal manufacturer.

The front exhibition space is a setting inviting different shop goers to witness an artist actively creating. You can find exhibits of heirloom quality lifestyle objects, such as primordially-shaped porcelain works placed sparingly on a hewn hardwood elongated table, or an off-centre arrangement of foraged flowers in blue handblown vases. Mjölk is as much a shop-house as it is a gallery, where the home and art collection is paired with the artists, who feed the soul through making.

What makes the household items so unique and exquisite is that Mjölk is in a category of design unto itself. Coaxing the art out from the interactions between tools and materials, Mjölk helps us reinterpret our daily rituals through a heightened beauty and aesthetic awareness.

Address 2959 Dundas Street West, Toronto, ON M6P 1Z2, +1 (416)551-9853, www.mjolk.ca, info@mjolk.ca | Getting there Subway to Dundas West (Line 2), then take 40 Junction bus to Dundas Street West at Pacific Avenue; by car, drive west on Dupont Street, merge right onto Dundas Street West | Hours Mon–Fri 10am–6pm, Sat 10am–5pm, Sun noon–5pm | Tip As Mjölk is to milk, sometimes you need a little crema in your coffee as you strike up a conversation with a 'Junctionite'. Crema Coffee has the bragging rights as the most fashionable café to grace the Junction area (3079 Dundas Street West, Toronto, ON M6P 1Z9, www.cremacoffee.ca).

72 — The Monkey's Paw

A random literary experience for a toonie

'Expect to be startled,' as owner Stephen Fowler says mischievously. The Monkey's Paw is a vintage bookstore that has the world's only automatic random book dispenser. Be careful what you attract into your life, because this is a place of bibliographic serendipity. The front display with steampunk aesthetic beckons you to explore the mysteries within. As you walk past the curated bookshelves displaying an eclectic array of rare nonfiction books, your head will be filled with unusual titles, beautiful tomes and collector's delights. At the back of the store is the coup de resistance: the Biblio-Mat. Designed and built by animation artist Craig Small, the Biblio-Mat is a stylish and unique alternative to the sidewalk discount bin. In fact, the book-vending machine was initially developed for a community festival and has developed an aura of lore with authors such as Neil Gaiman and Margaret Atwood.

Put in your toonie (two-dollar coin) and hear the noises from a past era. Listen to the hopeful rumble of the machine, the antique telephone ring and the satisfying slap of a book dropping into the receptacle. So, is the book that you are holding part of a past era? One would argue that a fine book, in the age of Amazon, AI and Google, has the same charm as the warmth of vinyl under a diamond shard needle. And which one did you get? Did you, like me, get a book called *Premarital Sexual Standards in America*, published in 1960? I never knew I was going to spend an hour bemused by dated, sincere observations.

From this strange used bookstore named after a supernatural short story written by W. W. Jacobs in 1902, your quest for discovery has begun. The Monkey's Paw is an excellent place for antiquarian book hunting. Here you can just accept the randomness of literary grace, and leave with new ideas and books you can put next to your vinyl collection.

Address 1267 Bloor Street West, Toronto, ON M6H 1N7, +1 (416)531-2123, www.monkeyspaw.com, wish@monkeyspaw.com | Getting there Subway to Lansdown (Line 2); 29 Dufferin bus to Dufferin; 47 Lansdowne bus to Wade Avenue | Hours Tue–Sat 11am–6pm, Sun noon–5pm | Tip Travel east on Bloor Street to Karelia Kitchen and you will find a Scandinavian gem of a restaurant, specializing in all things smoked as well as pastries (1194 Bloor Street West, Toronto, ON M6H 1N2, www.kareliakitchen.com).

73_Native Child and Family Services Longhouse

A healing place that comes from Indigenous 'ways of knowing'

Residential schools were government-sponsored religious boarding schools set up throughout 13 provinces to assimilate Indigenous children into Euro-Canadian society. These institutions caused unparalleled loss and pain in the Indigenous community and culture. When the children returned to their lands, they didn't know 'how to be'. They had lost connections to their family, community and Indigenous ways.

Native Child and Family Services of Toronto (NCFST) is a provincially designated children's aid society and is aboriginally governed. Because this is the first urban agency, the executive director, Elders, community members and architects retreated to Curve Lake, a reservation outside of Peterborough, to begin designing a traditional longhouse. Modeled after *Anishinaabe*, meaning the spirit that is lowered down from above, this healing space would be placed inside the agency's building downtown.

Cocoon-like and much longer than it is wide, the Indigenous Longhouse is made of yellow birch heartwood and eastern white cedar. You enter through a black portal. The floor is patterned, reminiscent of traditional matting. Medicines such as cedar, sweetgrass, sage and tobacco were placed under the floor. Dimmable light fixtures hang on red cables, coaxing the feeling of the element fire. Ceremony and blessings ask for continued guidance from the ancestors and reconnection in this spiritual place. The Longhouse is a sacred space of becoming, or 'coming to know', the Indigenous knowledge that is *experienced* through cultural elements, interpretation of stories, drumming and ceremonies. Community emerges from the relationships among these elements.

Experience the Longhouse by calling for an appointment. NCFST also has a green roof that grows sage, cedar, tobacco and sweetgrass.

Address 30 College Street West, Toronto, ON M5G 1K2, +1 (416)969-8510, www.nativechild.org, info@nativechild.org | Getting there Subway to College (Line 1) | Hours By appointment only | Tip Visit Taber Hill in Scarborough, the only First Nations ossuary protected as a cemetery in Canada. It is a site where approximately 500 Wyandot (Huron) Indigenous people are buried. It is marked by a mound and plaque with a moving poem written by Whitecloud, an Iroquois leader (Indian Mound Crescent, Scarborough, ON M1H 1W2, www.torontoist.com/2015/02/historicist-the-tabor-hill-ossuary).

74 Ontario Spring Sake Company

Saying 'kampai' in the distillery district

The Toronto distillery company Gooderman and Worts was at one point the largest manufacturer of spirits in the world. In the late 1860s, the company was also the largest national corporate taxpayer. The 19th-century industrial glory of this distillery's setting was polished up at the beginning of the 21st century to create a new showcase destination. What better environment to develop a Japanese sake brewery specializing in ancient techniques?

Ken Valvur, president of the Ontario Spring Sake Company, had already established a reputation for bringing Japanese culture to Canada by introducing Japanese food. He had spotted the bento box trend in the late 90s in London and translated it into the second-largest sushi brand on the continent. As a Torontonian of Estonian heritage with a passion for Japanese culture, it seemed only natural that for his next act he would start a sake brewing company. Setting up the company in an old limestone building, he was guided by a traditional brewmaster as to how best to brew small batches of unpasteurized sake. The brewmaster, or *toji*, was introduced to Ken by his advisors at the 350-year-old Miyasaka Brewing Co. in Japan.

Ken knew that the delicious, unpasteurized style of sake could never be imported to Canada, since the warehousing of the LCBO and the SAQ in Quebec is not refrigerated. By making it locally, he ensured that these delicious sakes can now be enjoyed at top Canadian restaurants and at the brewery store's tasting bar.

Using spring water from Muskoka and cedar from British Columbia, these sake brewers will show you how they blend local ingredients with ancient Japanese know-how on their tours. Bring your friends along and enjoy the coziness of a cup of sake delivered with Japanese hospitality. *Kampai!*

Address 55 Mill Street, Toronto, ON M5A 3C4, +1 (416)365-7253, www.ontariosake.com, info@ontariosake.com | **Getting there** 504 King streetcar to Cherry Street | **Hours** Sun–Thu noon–6pm, Fri & Sat noon–7pm | **Tip** Opened in 2017, the Spirit of York in the distillery district restored the Gooderman and Worts historic distillation buildings and made them into a steampunk contemporary architectural gem. They sell signature beverages made from their vodkas and gins (12 Trinity Street, Toronto, ON M5A 3C4, www.spiritofyork.com).

75 __ Osgoode Hall's Great Library
Toronto's hidden bibliographic beauty

Tucked away at the corner of Toronto's busy University Avenue and Queen Street is an elegant oasis. You exhale as you magically pass through the iron kissing gates, originally designed to keep out problematic farm animals, into what seems to be another era. You have entered the Osgoode Hall compound, the legal soul of Ontario, and the Law Society of Upper Canada, the governing body of Ontario's legal profession since 1832. Explore the exterior of the Palladian-style building and its tree-shaded gardens before entering inside.

Arriving through the tarnished front doors of this unheralded gem, wind your way through to the second floor. What awaits is the Great Library, one of the most breathtaking rooms in Toronto and an active study and reference area that houses over 120,000 legal volumes, the largest of its kind in Canada. Interesting even to mere mortals outside of the legal profession, take time to marvel at this architectural delight, juxtaposed against the melting pot of the various generations and ethnicities of law students all representing the Canada of today. The mesmerizing, ornate plaster ceiling of the Great Library is graciously supported by numerous ornamental columns. The cork floors, etched glass windows and cornucopia of volumes conjure up feelings of great pomp and history. A large fireplace and a World War I memorial serve as focal points at the ends of the room. Adjacent to the Great Library is an equally stunning American Room. This smaller, intimate space has warm wood features and is surrounded by 40 feet of floor-to-ceiling bookshelves. An elevated platform is reached by a winding spiral staircase for accessing the legal tomes on the second floor.

This bibliographic Temple of Justice is not to be missed. It would be almost 'criminal' not to include this fine example of Victorian Classical architecture on any tour of Toronto.

Address 130 Queen Street West, Toronto, ON M5H 2N6, +1 (416)947-3300, www.lsuc.on.ca/osgoode-hall | **Getting there** Subway to Osgoode (Line 1); 501 Queen streetcar to Queen Street West at York Street; 6 Bay bus to Bay Street at Queen Street West | **Hours** Mon – Fri 8:30am – 5pm | **Tip** The Osgoode Hall Restaurant's fare is delicious and well-priced. It is open 11:45am – 2pm from September until June (www.osgoodehallrestaurant.com).

76 Otto's Berlin Döner

Don't push the big blue button

Inside Toronto's young edgy multicultural market village of Kensington, one can find a little piece of Berlin. Each rung in the market's history has been dominated by one ethnic group or another, so that today's mosaic reveals the food and wares of vastly different cultures that have been collecting through the ages. Walking down the street, you understand that Kensington Market and all its small village bohemian charm is in perpetual resistance to Toronto's big steel building boom.

Former French fencer Thomas Masmejean and his partners were drawn to this neighbourhood a couple of years ago. They had hopes of finding a location for their electronic music nightclub but ended up with a successful café instead. Before Otto's Berlin Döner opened, Thomas and his chef flew to Berlin and Istanbul and ate 24 *döners* in 4 days. This dedication to the Berlin ouevre is apparent as you step into the lemon yellow neon lit cafe with industrial grey walls, which feel cheery even on a dull day. A mural of Berlin with graphically rendered iconic buildings greets you on your left, and the straightforward board menu offers delicious Turkish / German meat sandwich style *döners* filled with spiced meat, slaw, currywurst and carbonated yerba mate. Just the seducing smells of the kitchen alone make you understand why this busy place has a reputation for fine ingredients and satisfying Berliner food.

When you ask, 'Where is the washroom, please,' you find yourself walking down well-worn wooden service stairs. You turn the corner and open the door and find an otherwise non descript *American Standard* bathroom complete with a wall-hung sink and the patina of basement grit. Oh, what is this large plastic blue button on the wall across from the toilet? You cannot help yourself. You MUST give this button a push. It now becomes apparent, that the desire of the owners to open up an electronic music dance club is still, oh, so very real.

Move your body to the pulsating light.

Address 256 Augusta Avenue, Toronto, ON M5T 2L9, +1 (647)347-7713, www.ottosdoner.com, eat@ottosdoner.com | **Getting there** 506 Carlton streetcar to Augusta Avenue; 510 Spadina streetcar to Nassau Street | **Hours** Sun – Thu noon – 9pm, Fri & Sat noon – 11pm | **Tip** Cross the street and wander in to discover this is no ordinary place, it's The Poetry Jazz Café (224 Augusta Avenue, Toronto, ON M5T 2L7, www.poetryjazzcafe.com).

77 Pacific Mall

Practically priced products and pandemonium

Tired of mundane shopping malls full of cookie-cutter storefronts and repetitive chain stores? Looking for an unusual retail experience? Well look no further. Pacific Mall is not a typical Toronto shopping centre. With over 500 stores and corridors named after Hong Kong streets, it reminds you of a Chinese market full of products and pandemonium.

Pacific Mall is North America's largest indoor Asian mall. Typical of an Asian market, the stores are small glass cubicles all jammed together in orderly sugar cube-like lines. You are transported to a shopping district in Guangzhou or Shanghai. Full of knockoff brands, wacky phone cases and bubble teas, it invades your senses. The noise, smells and chaos are endless. Turning a corner and finding yet another Hello Kitty embossed phone case, you'll feel certain you are having déjà vu or are completely lost, yet again. The incredible density and repetitive corridors leave you consistently disoriented.

With a plethora of security guards in high-tech gear you are reminded of the many high-profile counterfeit and bootlegging raids that have occurred in the mall's buildings. Ding Dong Snacks, on the ground floor, is full of Japanese snacks, from Pocky sticks to Moomin cookies. This store, one of the longest standing retailers in the mall, is named after a popular Japanese cartoon character that has an endless supply of interesting treasures in his pockets. It is appropriate that Ding Dong retails many uniquely flavoured Japanese Kit Kats. Matcha green, perhaps? Heading upstairs to the food court, you are confronted with an array with smells and options. The array of hot pots, handmade noodles and other Asian treats is overwhelming. For moving beyond the mundane or looking for a unique Toronto experience while repairing your phone screen or purchasing a practically priced karaoke box, look no further than Pacific Mall.

Address 4300 Steeles Avenue East, Markham, ON L3R 0Y5, +1 (905)470-8785, www.pacificmalltoronto.ca | **Getting there** From downtown Toronto, take the Don Valley Parkway north, take provincial Route 404 north to 22, take a right on Steeles Avenue to Kennedy Road | **Hours** Sun–Thu 11am–8pm, Fri & Sat 11am–9pm | **Tip** For another uniquely Asian experience stop by Uncle Tetsu's Cheesecake. Located on the south side of Pacific Mall, the recipe was first developed in the Hakata area of Fukuoka, Japan. This creamy light cheesecake is a favourite with everyone (www.uncletetsu-ca.com).

78_ The Pasture

Bovine oasis amid a granite forest

In the frenzied tempo of Toronto's Financial District, you can find tranquil repose in a place where time is frozen. The Pasture, created by famous sculptor Joe Fafard, features seven life-sized bronze cows in various patinas that graze in a grassy courtyard.

What a juxtaposition! The cows are a lighthearted, peaceful counterpoint to the black modernist towers designed by Mies van der Rohe. They remind the often-harried passerby to slow down and put their hurries and their worries into perspective.

The TD Centre was where Toronto's towering skyline began in 1967. It was a time of great hope for Canada's future during this centennial year. In fact, Van der Rohe's architecture was the granddaddy of Toronto's future office towers. Toronto's monolithic structures are all built by machines; nothing is visceral. Presently, the ethereal, split-second data movement generated by computers and other machines seems transient. Very little is done by hand. The Pasture serves as a constant reference to how Toronto used to look when it was once called Muddy York. It exemplifies also how many Canadians got their start from humble origins.

Joe Fafard was born in a log house, one of 12 children, and helped his father farm the land. 'It was to a great degree normal, to make things with one's hands… at one time one milked the cows by hand, one studied anatomy without knowing it.' His offhand study of anatomy with farm work and butchery served him well. Fafard was named an Officer of the Order of Canada in 1981 for his outstanding contribution to the arts.

Don't be shy, there are no charging bulls here, just lounging cows on a pasture. You can mingle with them the courtyard, and enjoy your lunch break in their midst. Whatever your perspective, The Pasture harkens you to slow down and think about what was, what is, and what could be in a peaceful calm.

Address 66 Wellington Street West, Toronto, ON M5K 1A1 | **Getting there** Subway to St. Andrews (Line 1); 6 Bay bus to Wellington Street | **Hours** Unrestricted | **Tip** If you like cow sculptures, check out the fantastical hybrid animal statues by Cynthia Short called *Remembered Sustenance*. These strange whimsical creatures are part bunny, part puppy and part cow (200 Wellington Street West, Toronto, ON M5V 3G7).

79 Pinky's Ca Phe

Vietnamese food meets 1970s American GI experience

The name Pinky's Ca Phe was inspired by the pink rouge on the cheeks of Vietnamese ladies working the restaurants in Vietnam that served the visiting American soldiers. Chef Leemo Han had used this imagery formed during his honeymoon travels in Vietnam as he scoured Toronto for the found art that would create the carefully orchestrated ambiance of this hidden gem serving Vietnamese street food.

Relying primarily on word of mouth, the establishment has been frequented by city restaurant workers in the know, foodies who inform other foodies, and the savvy urban explorer who delights in the thrill of city scavenger hunts. Pinky's is found on a quiet residential street in a nondescript Victorian home with no signage. As you walk up the steps, you are greeted by GI Joe comic books that become the aesthetic radar for the whole dining experience. It is easy to forget the chilling winds of Toronto when you think you are sitting in Vietnam in a tropical roadside bar/eatery in the 1970s, intimately sharing dishes and cocktails in a crowded restaurant with dim lighting and tightly arranged seating.

This Canadian-Korean restauranteur grew up in Philadelphia, which is home to one of the largest Vietnamese populations on the East Coast. Growing up with American cultural portrayals of the Vietnam experience, coupled with a deep family passion for food, made this unusually blended restaurant a natural fit for Han. Menu specialties include 'You Dip, I Dip' Pho beef, tiger's milk ceviche, Han's marrow beef and mango papaya salad topped with grilled squid. Even the beverages are Vietnamese inspired, with the bartenders using FOCO Locos juices found in Asian grocery stores. And do not underestimate the pleasant power and punch of the signature cocktail, the Pink Lady. It's a perfect place to bring a date, and snuggle into a hidden portal of another time and place.

Address 53 Clinton Street, Toronto, ON M6G 2Y4, www.instagram.com/Pinkys_Caphe | Getting there 506 College streetcar to Clinton Street; by car, midway between Ossington Avenue and Bathurst Street | Hours Mon–Sat 6pm–2am | Tip You're in Little Italy, so if you wish to eat an Italian gourmet meal in another charming restaurant snuggled into Clinton Street, visit Giancarlo. It's a favourite with many Italian food fans (41 Clinton Street, Toronto, ON M6J 2N9, giancarlotrattoria.com).

80 Prehistoria

Recycling prehistoric antiquities

Imagine the Inuit hunters have just finished feasting on the meat of a newly caught narwhal and have tossed the remaining skull with its unique, unicorn-like tusk into a snowy garbage heap. This is where Ben Lovatt comes in, owner of Prehistoria. Ben, a former wildlife conservationist, states, "I made a jump from live animals to dead animals. I wanted to recycle them as art instead of letting them rot away." This theme of salvaging and recycling is apparent in every item of his shop and attached free museum. For Ben, managing Prehistoria is not a job but a calling. Where else can customers come to view such oddities of nature such as a narwhal skull with two tusks and have Ben generously explain the story behind it?

He sources his rare and unusual artefacts from zoos, vets and global Indigenous tribes, and has a very contentious relationship with Canada Customs. What would you do if you were shipping a 60-million-year-old fossilized crocodile from Morocco, and it came to you in pieces? Thank goodness Ben also does restoration work.

Prehistoria displays not only bones. In addition to palaeontology, you can find geological specimens, ancient relics, taxidermied animals, human skulls/bones, and macabre curiosities. If you are interested in civilizations of the past, you can purchase Viking jewelry, Roman glass, a Sumerian cuneiform tablet or a Tibetan necromancer mask. This adorned skull with ornate metal work can be yours for $15,000. Or you can just step in and explore the fascinating museum at no charge.

In an otherwise nondescript area of Toronto, you will find Prehistoria, the only shop of its kind in Canada. If you're into archeology, dinosaurs, anatomy, ancient civilizations or zoology, then Prehistoria is well worth a visit. Ben's contagious enthusiasm and storytelling adds new life to these old relics.

How Do You Measure Up?

Woolly Mammoth Leg

Did you know Woolly Mammoths roamed ancient Canada? This is a museum casting (reproduction) of a mammoth femur bone! You also have a femur bone in your leg, connecting from your knee to your hip.

Can you imagine how tall this mammoth would have been?

Do Not Lean On This Bone

Address 1193 Weston Road, Toronto, ON M6M 4P6, +1 (416)709-6777, www.prehistoria.ca | **Getting there** Subway to Eglinton (Line 1), then take 32 Eglinton West bus to Weston Road; by car, drive west from midtown on Eglinton and turn north on Weston Road | **Hours** Fri–Sun noon–6pm or by appointment | **Tip** If you are flying into Toronto and arriving at Pearson Airport Terminal 1, don't miss the prehistoric dinosaur installation piece, compliments of the Royal Ontario Museum.

81___ The Queen Streetcar

Write your own urban story on Route 501

The Queen Streetcar runs like a red streak through the collective memory of all long-time Toronto residents. Everyone has their story, something that happened to them on the streetcar, or an adventure where the streetcar was part of the plot. The ride, so long, so iconic, is one that is used by people to think things through, have a languid crosstown ride without going subterranean, or just have their own window onto the city while in transit. It can be a wistful ride, or a raucous one, especially when colourful passenger groups board the electric streetcar immersed in their day. It is the longest streetcar ride in North America, almost 25 kilometres in length, and one of the longest ones in the world. As many as 60,000 passengers climb on board daily.

This Red Rocket transports you through time. It follows Toronto's history of amalgamating various villages: The Beaches, Leslieville, and Parkdale, to name a few. The 501 route starts east at Neville Park, and ends at Long Branch. Each of the ends of the route takes the rider close to Lake Ontario, and the middle section through the densest part of the city. And at the halfway mark of the ride, you will find the cluster of old and new city hall buildings beside Nathan Phillips Square, the municipal heart of the city.

As the Toronto Transit Commission, better known as the TTC, states in its motto, taking public transit is 'The better way.' It can certainly be that, if you wish to explore a fascinating cross section of the urban core for the price of a streetcar ticket. Buy a day pass and explore many of these 111 places in Toronto that are situated along Queen Street.

The whizz of the electric motor, the clang of the bell, the faces of the passengers as they climb on board, the smell of well-worn floors and seats, and the passing panorama of cityscapes all provide a collage of experiences.

Address Board at any time along the route between Lake Shore Boulevard West and Queen Street East, www.ttc.ca/Routes/501/RouteDescription.jsp?tabName=map | Getting there See website for stations | Hours Mon–Sat 6am–1:30am, Sun 8am–1:30am | Tip Ride across the Toronto harbour with the ferry to the Toronto Islands. It is a perfect way to see yet another perspective of our Great Lakes city (9 Queens Quay West, Toronto, ON M5J 2H3, www.torontoisland.com).

82 __ The Real Jerk

Caribbean restaurant serves food and culture

The opening sequence shot for Rihanna and Drake's video 'Work' reveals the front signage of The Real Jerk. It is the only restaurant in Toronto that continues to have this type of exposure, as part of the rappers' video, with almost one billion views to date. Rihanna and Drake, the number one female and the number one male rapper in the world respectively, chose this setting for their video because of its authentic Jamaican vibe.

The owners, Lily and Ed Pottinger, have a passion for Jamaican food that started in their childhood, and Lily still follows traditional recipes. To accompany the copious selection of generously served meals, the restaurant also has an extensive list of rums. You can sip a Red Stripe beer or cocktail, eat jerk chicken or oxtail stew, listen to reggae/rap music and relax into this laid-back West Indian atmosphere in a decor reminiscent of Jamaican beachside restaurants. Toronto winter weather becomes a distant memory in this tropical setting. Ed Pottinger says, 'We don't just sell food, we sell culture.' And who goes for that culture? Toronto's very own Drake, who often drops in to pick up take out.

Drake is unequivocally Toronto's cultural ambassador, who has climbed up pop charts and even surpassed The Beatles with sales of hit singles. He has done this without forgetting the town that he has come from, and affectionately calls it 'The 6ix'. For some around the world, Toronto did not exist until our homeboy Drake put it on the map. He sings about it, he lives it, he supports the NBA Raptors, and makes viral videos here with his unabashed love of this city. The Real Jerk is a 'real good' fit for Drake.

Look for the sunshine logo on the restaurant sign in the southeast end of Toronto and let it serve as your beacon. Settle into the experience of home cooking served up with Jamaican hospitality, and lose your stress from work work work.

Address 842 Gerrard Street East, Toronto, ON M4M 1Y7, +1 (416)463-6055, www.therealjerk.com, therealjerk@therealjerk.com | **Getting there** 501 Queen streetcar east to Carlaw Avenue | **Hours** Sun 2–10pm, Mon & Tue 11:30am–10pm, Wed 11:30am–11pm, Thu 11:30am–12:30pm, Fri 11:30–1am, Sat noon–1am | **Tip** Looking for dessert? Travel west on Gerrard Street East to Wong's Ice Cream and try their black sesame and salted duck egg or wasabi honey ice cream. Contribute to this Instagram sensation (617 Gerrard Street East, Toronto, ON M4M 1Y2, www.wongsicecream.com).

83 __ The Rooster Coffee House

Rise and shine, it's coffee time

Gracefully perched on top of a hill adjacent to Riverdale Park, on a somewhat sleepy part of Broadview Avenue, is the Rooster Coffee House. The Rooster stands alone on a mostly residential street, a strange twist that makes it a perfect hangout for both local neighbours and inquisitive coffee explorers. This indie coffee shop, complete with bright red umbrellas and striped black and white awnings, makes you smile, knowing you will love this place well before you have even graced its coffee counter.

Co-owners Shaun Andrews and Dave Watson now have three Rooster locations across the city. However, the Broadview Rooster rises, or crows, above the rest, having won many accolades over the years including best café in the city. Jim Cuddy from Toronto's own Blue Rodeo describes hanging out at the Rooster with his wife, sipping on lattes and chatting with friends, as his idea of a perfect Saturday. It is a neighbourhood pub with an eclectic collection of furniture that feels as if you are walking into someone's French-inspired, shabby-chic living room. The walls are decorated with bulletins of upcoming events, obituaries of wonderful Torontonians and random thoughts for all to ponder.

Join the line up with the locals as the baristas work fast and furiously while calmly chatting to friendly and familiar clientele. Regulars are clear that the delicious consistency of the Rooster's beverages is what keeps them coming back in droves. The drinks are dreamy and so creamy and rich that sugar doesn't even cross your mind. The brewed coffee, specialty teas, local juices and pastries round out the experience.

Consider taking your frothy latte and wander across to the park, positioning yourself on front row seats to take in the Toronto skyline. Whether you are in need of a quick cup of java or a deliciously, loungy afternoon, stop by and join the local flock at The Rooster.

Address 479 Broadview Avenue, Toronto, ON M4K 2N4, +1 (416)995-1530, www.roostercoffeehouse.com | **Getting there** Dundas streetcar 505 to Broadview Avenue at Withrow Avenue; 506 Carlton streetcar to Gerrard Street East at Broadview Avenue | **Hours** Daily 7am–7pm | **Tip** Take in the sunset or cross the street and enjoy great views of the Toronto skyline from Riverdale Park East (550 Broadview Avenue, Toronto, ON M4K 2N6).

84 Ryerson Image Centre

Iconic photojournalism from a starring collection

What was once a brewery warehouse has been transformed into a high-tech architectural wonder. The Ryerson Image Centre plays on the theme of light and motion, reflecting the essence of film and photography. The exterior LED lighting changes like a kaleidoscope of colour, illuminating this educational photo-art museum and reference library. The main floor is home to a world-class photo gallery with new collections exhibited every couple of months. It invites students and connoisseurs to explore the boundless permeations of photographic art excellence.

During the day, when the LED light show is not on display, the building's facade showcases the most important roster of Canada's who's who list. Fourteen bold black-and-white photographs present portraitures of our nation's greats in the fields of the arts, sports, science, academics and politics. These include: Margaret Atwood, John Candy, Leonard Cohen, Chief Dan George, Wayne Gretzky, Karsh, K. D. Lang, Marshall McLuhan, Oscar Peterson, Mary Pickford, Buffy Sainte-Marie, David Suzuki, and Pierre Trudeau. Each enlarged photo is from the Black Star Photo Collection, the true star of the Ryerson Image Centre.

Ryerson University is nationally famous for film and photography, and also for its cutting-edge journalism program. So it's only befitting that The Black Star Collection has found a permanent home here. This photojournalism agency, started by German refugees in New York City in the 1920s, was internationally celebrated for introducing new techniques in photography and illustrated journalism. This vast collection includes almost 300,000 images, which were used by magazines such as *LIFE* and *Time*. An appointment is necessary to view these treasures.

Photography documents so much more than selfies; it records our global history and all of its exciting major shifts. The Black Star collection will not disappoint.

Address 33 Gould Street, Toronto, ON M5B 1W1, +1 (416)979-5164, ryersonimagecentre.ca, ric@ryerson.ca | **Getting there** Subway to Dundas (Line 1) | **Hours** Tue 11am–6pm, Wed 11am–8pm, Thu & Fri 11am–6pm, Sat & Sun noon–5pm | **Tip** On the other side of the RIC building, go and have a coffee at Balzac's. The coffee is fantastic, and black star tiles on the floor will remind you why you came here (www.balzacs.com/locations/ryerson-image-arts).

85__Sally the Elephant
An unforgettable lawn ornament

Typically, lawn ornaments go unnoticed – perhaps a hidden garden troll, a kitschy concrete bird or a miniature pagoda. However, a street in Toronto's Junction has a different vision for the average garden gnome. Tucked away on a nondescript street near the Christie Pits lives Sally, a 10-foot, white Indian elephant occupying the entirety of the home's front garden. Sally, who has inhabited the garden since 2003, has a solemn, almost meditative look. Although she may have seen better days, Sally most certainly has some wisdom to share.

Elephants in general are representative of honor and stability and a white elephant is a true rarity and a sacred symbol of royal brawn. In the Hindu religion, the elephant is found in the form of the deity Ganesh who is revered as the remover of life's obstacles and the deva of fortune and wisdom. In 1999, Sally was a thesis project created by Matt Donovan while attending the Ontario College of Art and Design. This beautifully tusked mammoth is created out of an artistic combination of chicken wire, fiberglass, plywood and spray foam. Donovan originally stored the post-thesis elephant in his parents' basement until James Lawson, a friend of Donovan's, agreed to gussy up his front garden with the Sally.

For her keepers, James and his very accommodating wife, Sally has become an iconic neighborhood fixture for East Annex residences. Over the years the Lawson's have been witness to many visitors and passersby. Although the majority of visitors and local residents are positive about Sally, the unorthodox, life-sized Toronto elephant takes on its own meaning to each visitor. For some, it's a place to worship, a place to meet or just a place to wonder. For others, it conjures up a playful, eclectic spirit evoking scenes of a cartoon character or a low-budget indie movie. Come visit and create your own interpretation.

Address 77 Yarmouth Road, Toronto, ON M6G 1X1 | Getting there 26 Dupont bus to Christie Street | Hours Unrestricted from the outside only | Tip The Ontario College of Art and Design is an incubator of new artists and designers and is Canada's largest and oldest institute for art and design. Visit the Sharp Centre for Design and see one of the most unique buildings in Toronto (100 McCaul Street, Toronto, ON M5T 1W1, www.ocadu.ca/about/sharp-centre-for-design.htm).

86 Sauce on the Danforth

Victorian-goth bordello-chic lounge

This saucy little lounge on the Danforth is a delightful reprieve for any bourbon drinking art lover. Sauce is a take off of a New Orleans bordello. Red is the predominant colour scheme that runs throughout this cozy, textured interior. Nude paintings adorn the walls with a high-class twist; they're all artworks created by the great masters including Manet, Ingres, and Titian. Not an art history major? No worries. Sauce provides an art reference book for clients to peruse and identify the various paintings and their genius creators. The bar counter itself acts like an encyclopedia of Western fine art treasures. Hundreds of postcard-sized prints under glass display everything from medieval art to Picasso and contemporary art.

Michelle, the owner, adds her own personal, creative flair to the environment. A large TV screen flashes unusual photos and other iconic cultural images addressing the current political discussions of the day. These visual compilations rotate every couple of months, and provide an interesting talking point to your new bar neighbour who might be sipping one of their on-tap craft beers. The beer offerings rotate throughout the seasons as well. Cocktails are served in vintage glassware, and it's been rumoured that some regular customers have claimed their own special glass hidden behind the bar.

The real shine to this ruby gem is the live music most nights of the week. It's a magnet for musicians of all stripes and types. The intimate space is more parlour room than concert hall, so the musical performances have a particular intimacy about them. Jazz, piano lounge music, pop and rock cover the music spectrum here at Sauce. If you're lucky, you might rub elbows with a celebrated local musician trying out new material. For steamy and saucy summer nights, you can sit on the front patio, or nestle into the private back patio with its own bar.

A perfect red-velvet hideaway any day of the week.

Address 1676 Danforth Avenue, Toronto, ON M4J 1M9, +1 (647)748-1376,
sauceonthedanforth.com | Getting there Subway to Coxwell (Line 2) | Hours
Mon–Thu 4pm–2am, Fri & Sun 3pm–2am, Sat 2pm–2am | Tip Just a couple of
doors away, visit Vii Design shop. The shop specializes in unique cushions and
one-of-a-kind giftware sourced locally, as well as from Estonia, Latvia, Portugal, Bali
and Nepal. The design sensibility of owner Viive will inspire you to leave toting a bag
(1434 Danforth Avenue East, Toronto, ON M4J 1N4, www.viidesigns.ca).

87 Shortstack Records
Acoustically high off vinyl fidelity

In the back of basement vintage clothing store The Black Market are rows of bins filled with vinyl treasures. Shortstack Records owner Cal McLean is not just a record peddler, but a seasoned curator of musical tastes, genres and fine musical recordings. Although he is a new owner of the used record store, he is a part of the growing one-billion-dollar-a-year vinyl industry. Vinyl records never went out of style to the young Cal who started collecting as a teenager in high school. Now, in this digital, downloading era, many others seem to agree. In fact, as vinyl record sales continue to grow, CD and downloading sales are declining.

As you browse and peruse the stacks with your fingers and your eyes, you can admire and appreciate the art of the album cover. You're already forming an intimate relationship with the record even before listening to the music. 'Vinyl allows you to have a tactile ownership with your music,' Cal points out when asked about the appeal of owning records and a turntable. There is also the thrill of the find. You can revisit your past with a copy of *The Dark Side of the Moon* or fill out your Mozart collection with a copy of the soundtrack to *Amadeus*. If you have an obscure request, or don't quite know what you are looking for, you can ask Cal.

That personable touch is what makes this record store more than just a purveyor of vinyl. Posters grace the walls of this otherwise garage outpost aesthetic, with the *High Fidelity* movie poster earning prime positioning.

Records bought and sold here are fairly priced, and the store has forged a well-deserved reputation from Toronto's music scene and media. McLean will, in his own words, 'shepherd' you through the vinyl experience. As the future unfolds, Cal and Shortstack Records are hoping to highlight the experiential value of vinyl, and ignite a passion for an authentic sound.

Address 256A Queen Street West, Toronto, ON M5V 1Z8, +1 (416)205-9191, www.shortstackrecords.com | Getting there Subway to Osgoode (Line 1); 501 Queen streetcar to John Street | Hours Mon–Sat noon–7pm, Sun noon–6pm | Tip Walk across the street and check out the illusory sculpture of a car exploding through the 3rd-floor brick wall (299 Queen Street West, Toronto, ON M5V 2Z5).

88 _ Scarborough Bluffs

Lake life on the edge

It's difficult to describe the Scarborough Bluffs in the east end of Toronto since there are many parts to the story, and many moving ones at that. The most important story is that the chalky white cliffs are increasingly eroding and creeping away from the shoreline of Lake Ontario as a response to human activity.

By visiting Scarborough Bluffs, you have an opportunity to move out of an urban Toronto experience into an environment displaying nature's colossal wonders. The chalky pale cliffs have been likened to the white cliffs of Dover, whereas explorers at the top of the cliffs taking in the grand vista view of Lake Ontario and its sandy shores compare the panorama to the coastline of the island of Malta.

Up above, as you explore the several kilometres of hiking paths that line the eroding cliffs, the Bluffs Lookout offers a spectacular view of Lake Ontario. Given that the cliffs are nearly 100 metres high, with crumbling cliff faces, it is impossible to walk down the steep slope to the shoreline. Conservation officials are rethinking how to provide the best cliff top experience while trying to mitigate the dangers to hikers and obviously slow down the erosion. Presently, you need to park in a residential area and make your way towards the cliffs through small residential parks. It is best to come equipped with hiking shoes, a respect for the local residents and a strong sense of adventure and heed to caution.

Below, Bluffer's Park offers public parking, a busier recreational beach with grassy picnic and barbeque areas. What type of experience you will have as you explore this east-end shoreline treasure will really depend on what level of adventure you are in the mood for. If you wish to take in the views and hikes from the top and explore the water's edge at the bottom of the cliffs on the same day, it's best to bring a car. Whatever your fancy, a day at the Bluffs is a day to remember.

Address 61 Under Cliff Drive, Toronto, ON M1N 3Z5, www1.toronto.ca/parks/prd/
facilities/complex/1748 | Getting there Subway to Kennedy (Line 2 & 3), then walk
30 metres to board 12 Kingston Road bus to Chine Drive, then a 1.1-kilometre / 0.7-mile
walk to Scarborough Bluffs Park; by car, take the Don Valley Parkway, exit O'Connor Drive
(which becomes) St. Clair Avenue East. Turn south on Brimley Road and continue until you
reach the Scarborough Bluffs Park. | Hours Dawn–dusk | Tip After exploring the top and
bottom of the Scarborough Bluffs, go visit the Dogfish Pub & Eatery by the marina at the
bottom of Bluffer's Park. There, you can enjoy the beauty of the lake as you sip and eat
(7 Brimley Road, Scarborough, ON M1M 3H3, www.thedogfish.ca).

89 South-Western Bathhouse

Banja, birch, borsht, beer and bathrobes

Like a Russian nesting doll, the unexpected treasure at the heart of the experience is the Russian *banja*. Within the Canadian suburban mini-mall, and within the Russian bathhouse tradition, you will find a hidden gem: a family's interpretation of an age-old cedar Russian hut, replete with rituals. Here, one has the opportunity to experience centuries-old beliefs and rituals associated with Russian folklore. To 'go to banja' was to give both your body and your soul a good cleaning, or detoxification. The wooden hut would have been located in a public place at the edge of a village, tended to by the village outlier. The Russian banya is considered a sacred place to this day, containing all the elements of nature: water, air, fire and earth.

Victor and Valentina Tourianski left Sochi, Russia in 2010 for Canada. They re-made the banya into a business, and lovingly reshelved their village collections and mixed antiques with their newer Slavic finds. Vintage Lenin propaganda posters, copper teapots, and large silver tea urns arranged along faux rafters adorn this detox space.

In between rounds of bathing, you rest and hydrate. Wrapped in a white waffle robe, resting until your body reaches room temperature, you can hydrate and wander through a series of rooms. In one room, you can drink tea or beer; in another, watch nature documentaries in dark rooms; in yet another, eat borsht and pickled vegetables. Order berries with medicinal vodka shots. Rest and return for the next round. Put on your felt sauna hat, and head in with soaking venik branches to whisk away your tensions.

This transported Black Sea banya feels right for channeling your inner bohemian spirit. It is not a spa. It is a social experience that unfolds through repeated rounds of bathing and mingling amongst provocative imagery of cultural artefacts, food and drink.

Address 2200 Dundas Street East, Mississauga, ON L4X 2V3, +1 (289)232-6088, www.banya.ca | Getting there Subway to Kipling (Line 2), transfer to 112 West Mall bus towards Disco Road to the West Mall Crescent at Dundas Street West (south side), access the entrance from the laneway that runs along the west side of the 2200 building | Hours Tue – Wed 4pm – midnight, Sat noon – midnight, Sun noon – 11pm | Tip If restoration of the soul is what you seek, check out the Russian Orthodox Christ the Saviour Cathedral (823 Manning Avenue, Toronto, ON M6G 2W7, www.christthesavioursobor.com).

90 __ St. Anne's Church
Saints and paints

Turning a corner off a busy street of Toronto's Brockton Village, you will find the unlikely setting of a Byzantine-style church. St. Anne's Anglican Church seamlessly illuminates fascinating tales of history and artistic creation produced by cultural visionaries who have helped define Canadian style on a world stage. While sitting in the pews, the most important theme that becomes evident is the story of the Christian faith, as interpreted by Canada's icons of fine art.

The church, built in 1905 – 1907, is a miniature model of the world-famous Byzantine church Hagia Sophia of Constantinople. After Reverend Skey's trip to Turkey, he hired Ford Howland, an architect, along with Edmund Burke, a specialist in Byzantine design, to build a bigger church for the growing congregation. Skey had only three criteria for the architect, 'The congregation needs to see me, hear me, and have lots of air.'

Before the Group of Seven became famous, the Reverend Skye asked J. E. H. MacDonald (the group's founder) to decorate his new church in 1923. MacDonald, in turn, recruited Fred Varley and Franklin Carmichael, also part of the Group of Seven, to paint the saints. Although the artists were asked to embrace the flat and two-dimensional style of Byzantine art, they still left their personal mark and individual flare.

You just need to look at the face of Isaiah to understand Varley's genius for self-expression. Each artist painted on canvas in their studio, and then brought their finished art to be permanently attached to the church walls. It's unique to view their art portraying religious themes, as their signature aesthetic collection celebrates the great Canadian outdoors.

The church in the present day is both a provincial and national heritage site, and it has a vibrant parish life. Come and sit with the saints, and enjoy some world-class Canadian art.

Address 270 Gladstone Avenue, Toronto, ON M6J 3L6, +1 (416)536-3160, www.saintanne.ca | **Getting there** 505 Dundas streetcar to Gladstone Avenue | **Hours** Worship services Sun 10:30am, Ministry Centre Mon–Thu 9:30am–12:30pm, tours first Sunday of month 11:45am | **Tip** If you are in the mood to go exploring historic Anglican churches, check out the Church of the Holy Trinity, which is surrounded by the Toronto Eaton Centre downtown. This old, yet progressive church hosts many cultural events in the city (10 Trinity Square, Toronto, ON M5G 1B1, www.holytrinitytoronto.org).

91 Sugar Beach

A contrived landscape that people are craving

Digging your toes into the granular sand of Sugar Beach transports you into the sweet and strange world of Willie Wonka. Set on a preexisting industrial pier where Jarvis Street meets Lake Ontario, the sparkling water carries a double reading, one of play and artifice, and the other of transport and production.

The parallel continues with the sand and sugar side by side, and the subtle burnt malt sweet odours combining the two. Claude Cormier, a Montreal artist, created a destination that is strikingly uncanny – a beach so familiar yet unknown. Sugar Beach is a triangular wedge of white sand, candy-floss pink fiberglass umbrellas, white Muskoka chairs, and constructed greenery arranged in a non-organic plan. There is even a candy-striped rock to climb. Did Mr. Wonka advise Claude Cormier how to keep it real in this manufactured land of artifice next to the sugar factory?

Sink yourself into a Muskoka chair, put on some sunscreen and rose-coloured sunglasses, and observe the industrial magic that is playing out in front of you. A massive freighter holding 20,000 tons of raw sugar has just come in after 20 days at sea from Brazil and is moored 50 metres away at the Redpath Sugar factory in front of you, making you feel as big as an Oompa Loompa. If you are fortunate, you will observe the grab bucket arm of the crane yawn open and scoop a massive amount of raw sugar straight out of the ship's hold. About seven tons of sugar per scoop are hoisted high, the dark blonde sugar spilling as it moves across and is dropped into a funnel-shaped hopper that leads to the bowels of the factory.

Cormier has, with the creation of Sugar Beach, revealed with his design what is already there. What is so historically real for the site, sugar and water, has been reinterpreted as an imaginative place to play. As Willie Wonka says, 'Being here you'll be free if you truly wish to be.'

Address 11 Dockside Drive, Toronto, ON M5A 1B6, +1 (416)338-4386 | Getting there Subway to Union (Line 1); 72 Pape bus to Queen's Quay East at Lower Jarvis Street | Hours Daily 8am–11pm | Tip Explore the journey of sugar from Brazil to your kitchen table by visiting the Redpath Sugar Museum (95 Queens Quay East, Toronto, ON M5E 1A3, www.museumsontario.ca/museum/Redpath-Sugar-Museum).

92 Sunnybrook Stables
Saddle up in the middle of Toronto

Hidden in the urban oasis of Sunnybrook Park are Toronto's own public English riding stables. The Kilgour Family purchased the 200-acre Sunnybrook country estate that invoked the spirit of a stately English manor in 1909. Major Joseph Kilgour was a prominent businessman, the owner of a paper box company, gentleman farmer and one of North America's most famous horsemen. The riding legacy continues as all types of equestrians are encouraged to saddle up, offering lessons for novice riders, summer camps for children, training for national competitors and various celebrated competitions.

Peering across the green baseball and soccer fields, imagine the regular fox hunts that travelled through the wooded hillsides following the Toronto Hunts Hounds. The original farm was home to one of the first indoor riding arenas in Canada with a viewing gallery that still exists today and complete with a minstrel section where leading musicians from far and wide would come to play. In addition to the show stable, the farm consisted of horse and cattle barns, a dairy, sheep pens, piggeries and a granary, all celebrating the Kilgour's love of both fine horses and farming.

Walking through Sunnybrook's many alluring paths and secret trails, you forget for a moment or two that you are actually in one of the largest metropolitan areas in North America. The Kilgour farm still remains the nucleus for this country park in the city. When Alice Kilgour gifted the farm over to the city in 1928, the land and buildings were said to be valued at a giveaway price of $350,000. The government has since used part of the land to open a modern hospital for Canadian veterans, the well-recognized Sunnybrook Health Centre. Absolutely worth a visit, the visionary parkland is a brilliant reminder of the Kilgour's 1928 gift of nature and a legacy to be enjoyed by generations of Torontonians.

Address 1132 Leslie Street, North York, ON M3C 3L7, +1 (416)444-4044, www.sunnybrookstables.ca | Getting there Subway to Eglinton (Line 1), then board the 54 Lawrence East bus, or the 51 Leslie bus to 1121 Leslie Street | Tip Hike one of the beautiful trails surrounding the stables. The winding Don River Trail is a welcome river refuge (www.donrivervalleypark.ca/things-to-do/the-trails).

93__ The Tarragon Theatre

Celebrating Canadian talent in a cribbage factory

It is wonderful to see the imagination of urban centres as they re-purpose abandoned factories for inspiring innovative purposes. This trend is becoming more prolific in Toronto, and leading the way in 1970 was a gem in Toronto's theatre world. The Tarragon Theatre, named after the founder's favourite herb, is a fabulous boutique the-atre company, which was once the site of an old cribbage factory and an alleged World War II fabricator. Founded by Jane and Bill Glass-co, the Tarragon is a departure from its roots of board games and co-vert assembly lines.

For a small theatre, the Tarragon has garnered great respect with its long history of producing iconic Canadian work. It is the biggest supporter of new Canadian playwrights in the country, supporting the careers of renowned creative talents such as David French and Jason Sherman. The Tarragon has held onto both a wide-reaching and loyal audience and the endorsement of government funding, quite a feat in the face of a precarious time in the theatre world.

Tucked amongst homes in the Tarragon Village, the theatre has a local sensibility. The Tarragon, with its ample parking and close prox-imity to restaurants and subways, provides a quiet urban reprieve. Walking into the Tarragon you feel immediately at home, perhaps akin to a neighbourhood coffee shop. The lobby is a friendly place with a well-appointed snack bar and walls proudly littered with pho-tographs of the Tarragon's tremendous talent.

The small theatre and sunken stage create an intimate setting you can share with the cast. The productions often provide a mirror into our lives. Richard Rose, the current artistic director, has been able to navigate a winning formula by pushing the boundaries and experimenting with new talent. Prepare to be engulfed by tragedy, joy and pathos. Come be swept away by remarkable new Canadian works and artists.

Address 30 Bridgman Avenue, Toronto, ON M5R 1X3, +1 (416)531-1827, www.tarrangontheatre.com | **Getting there** Subway to Dupont (Line 1), then walk northeast 0.5 kilometres until you reach Tarragon theatre | **Hours** Visit website for season performance schedule | **Tip** For a nice meal beside the Tarragon, try Fat Pasha, a funky eatery with country-chic decor serving Middle Eastern and Jewish dishes (414 Dupont Street, Toronto, ON M5R 1V9, www.fatpasha.com).

94 Tea at the Royal York

A salute to Toronto's grand old dame

To quote Henry James, 'There are few hours in life more agreeable than the hour dedicated to the ceremony known as afternoon tea.' So relax into this British colony, feel like a king or queen and enjoy some tea at Toronto's regal Royal York Hotel. The state-of-the-art Royal York opened in 1929 in what was one of Toronto's most glittery social occasions. This *Canadian Castle* was the tallest and most luxurious hotel in the British Commonwealth at the time, complete with private radios, showers and bathtubs in each of its 1,000-plus rooms. There was a handset in every room with a 60-foot-long signature telephone switchboard requiring 35 full-time operators. With many famous and distinguished patrons, it was a true cause célèbre.

The grand old dame's afternoon cream tea is complete with warm scones, fresh clotted cream, an assortment of jams and loose-leaf teas. This elegant experience takes place in the stately, wood-panelled, bookshelf-lined Library Room. It is a quintessential, hidden-away hotel bar with a calm, serene vibe perfect for conversation and connection. Sink into the comfy chairs as teapots, cakes and canopies fly at you from all directions. Perhaps try the Queen's favourite Creamy Earl Grey Tea. If you need a little more, there is also a wide assortment of classic cocktails from which to choose. Consider periodically pausing from your tea and rewinding time to imagine a majestic period in Toronto's history.

Although the experience is appetizingly approachable, it would be negligent not to review teatime manners. Similar to patrons of London's Claridge's, extend your pinkie finger, add your milk after the tea has been poured and eat finger sandwiches with your hands, the Devon cream is applied first with the jam tastefully on top. An afternoon to remember, come honour Toronto's British roots and important sipping and noshing rituals.

Address 100 Front Street West, Toronto, ON M5J 1E3, +1 (416)860-5004, www.fairmont.com/royal-york-toronto/dining/afternoontea | Getting there Subway (Line 1), UP Express, VIA Rail, or Go Transit to Union, exit to Front Street | Hours Sat & Sun seatings at noon, 12:30pm, & 2:30pm, Mon–Wed 2:30pm | Tip Be sure to take advantage of the free historical tour of the hotel following your indulgent afternoon tea. Weather permitting, venture upstairs and visit the three beehives on the hotel's breath-taking rooftop garden. It's a treat not to be missed.

95_ Terrence Donnely Centre
Bamboo boulevard for brainiacs

A glass-inspired wedge of architectural wonder has been built between two historic buildings, just off College Street at the University of Toronto and connecting the research buildings and many scientific disciplines. The Donnely Centre for Cellular and Biomolecular Research allows graduate researchers in biology, computer science, engineering, and biochemistry to explore new boundaries of DNA and gene splicing, all under one roof. Opened in 2005, the world-class genome research coming from this collaboration is not the only gem to be found in this building.

On the western side of the building, a stunning bamboo forest lines the walkway through the research centre. Fed by sunlight pouring through the atrium, this old bamboo forest gives winter-weary Torontonians a true visual and olfactory burst of glorious green chlorophyll. The bamboo is stunningly displayed against the backdrop of the golden-brick mining building built in the 1800s. Little stepping stones lead to wooden platforms carefully placed in the middle of the verdant foliage to create sitting areas surrounded by green on all sides. Breathe in the air of the green building that is naturally filtered and humidified by the growing biome. Above the bamboo forest is an interconnected walkway for the lofty scientists to walk from lab to lab, look below and connect with the earth.

Mere mortals are encouraged to use the building as well. A coffee shop and restaurant can be found at the end of the walkway, where you can rub elbows with some of Canada's top researchers. You are invited to use the stepping stones that lead to the sitting areas so that you too can perch yourself.

The Donnely Centre is a far cry from the sterile white lab rooms of yesteryear, and the bamboo boulevard serves as a reminder to everyone walking through that we are all stewards of Planet Earth and all its inhabitants.

Address 160 College Street, Toronto, ON M5S 3E1, +1 (416)978-8287, tdccbr.med.utoronto.ca/image-gallery | Getting there Subway to Queen's Park (Line 1), then walk 160 metres west | Hours Daily 8am–5pm | Tip The 'Insulin: Toronto's Gift to the World' display in the MaRS building on the south side of College is a joint effort of the Faculty of Medicine, the MaRS Discovery commercialization initiative and the University Health Network. Follow the discoveries that changed the world for diabetics (www.utoronto.ca/news/celebrating-90-years-insulin).

96 Textile Museum of Canada

Perhaps a little woven retail therapy?

If you are a true aficionado of fabrics and fashion, then do we have a place for you! Located slightly off of the beaten path, in what appears to be a three-story apartment building, lives a hidden textile treasure. The Textile Museum of Canada is a small, niche museum that is big on beauty and colour. Unlike the mammoth ROM or AGO, you feel as if you might wrap your arms around the exhibits in less than a couple of hours. Renowned internationally for its diverse and relevant exhibits in addition to its innovative programming, a visit here is both educational and entertaining.

It is fascinating to realize that the history of clothing and textiles and the technology behind them is really a reflection of human history and civilizations. The wearing of clothing, a uniquely human characteristic, was originally used to protect from the cold, heat and rain. It is unknown exactly when humans began wearing clothing though anthropologists believe that vegetation and animal skins became more common as humans migrated to new northern climates.

As you enter the building, you are greeted by some of the 14,000 carefully curated textiles that compose the collection from Canada and around the world. All pieces seem to portray both a textile and human story. Both the permanent and rotating exhibits of fabrics, garments, carpets and ceremonial cloths celebrate the 2,000 years of textile history. The museum's rotating exhibits change throughout the calendar year and are full of local, Canadian and international artists. Become a textile anthropologist as you bathe in the colour, textiles and their cultural manifestations. Finally, for some retail therapy, make sure not to miss the gift shop, a true rose within the garden. Full of bright-coloured woven computer covers or soothing coffee-table books celebrating Chinese silks, you are certain to find a special something.

Address 55 Centre Avenue, Toronto, ON M5G 2H5, +1 (416)599-5321,
www.textilemuseum.ca | Getting there Subway to St. Patrick (Line 1), then walk
southeast in the direction of the Textile Museum | Hours Daily 11am–5pm, Wed
11am–8pm | Tip Visit the 3D TORONTO sign, an illuminated three-dimensional
sign in Nathan Phillip's Square that spells the city's name. At 72 feet in length and lit
by LED lights, it can create an estimated 228 million colour combinations. Originally
installed for the 2015 Pan American Games as a temporary attraction, the city decided
to continue to operate the sign after it became popular with tourists and residents.

97 — The Tollkeeper's Cottage

The birthplace of urban sprawl

Carefully navigating the city's streets with the latest traffic app, it is intriguing to imagine the birthplace of Toronto's traffic. In the 1800s, when the Toronto area was better known as Upper Canada, private companies were contracted to manage the primitive corduroy, log-based road systems. As Toronto was largely covered in forest, it was almost impossible to travel from one community to another. With no tax base, the private toll companies funded the modern roadways, and thus began Toronto's urban sprawl. Levies were charged – sixpence for every vehicle drawn by two horses plus or minus adjustments for asses or mules.

Davenport Road, Toronto's oldest road, had five tollgates. Tollgate Number Three also included the cottage to house the tollkeeper and his family. Despite the cramped and often harsh cottage quarters, frequently with meat and vegetables hanging on the ceiling to survive the long winters, this small cabin was home to 4–5 consecutive families. An unattractive vocation, the tollkeepers, often Irish immigrants, would have to make up the difference if passers did not pay their fees. The cottage is believed to be the only surviving tollgate existing in Canada today.

This unassuming historical treasure has been relocated many times but the city granted this permanent location when the land ceased to be a TTC turnaround site. The Community History Project restored and now owns and operates the tollhouse. With the magical cooperation of 50 local residents, using a very modest budget, they began an intricate restoration process and marked the cottage an official heritage site. The cottage is furnished to represent the 1860s, when a family of nine lived in these tiny quarters. Complete with its original floorboards and thick vertically planked walls, we are taken back in time to the beginnings of Toronto's traffic history.

Address 750 Davenport Road, Toronto, ON M6G 2V5, +1 (416)515-7546, www.tollkeeperscottage.ca, tollkeeperscottage@gmail.com | **Getting there** Subway to Spadina (Line 1 & 2), then take the 127 Davenport West bus, to Davenport Road at Bathurst Street; 7 Bathurst bus to Davenport Road | **Hours** Sat 11am–4pm in the winter, 11am–5pm in the summer | **Tip** Visit Artscape adjacent to the Wychwood Barns, located in an old streetcar repair facility. It is a self-sustaining community of artists and non-profit organizations, with a wonderful art gallery (601 Christie Street, Toronto, ON M6G 4C7, www.torontoartscape.com).

98__TIFF Bell Lightbox

Beam like a celebrity on the moving red carpet

The history of the red carpet, the colour of romance, rage and radiance, extends back centuries. Oriental carpets in Renaissance paintings, although patterned, often featured red as the predominant background colour. Today's red carpet is the symbol of celebrity at the Academy Awards, and also at Toronto's International Film Festival (TIFF). If you are hankering to feel regal and celebrated, Toronto's Bell Lightbox's red escalator is open to us all. Come celebrate your own effervescence and ride the moving red staircase – the nucleus of the city's vibrant film culture.

TIFF's 10-day movie festival is the kick-off to the prestigious movie season. TIFF is known as one of the world's most well-attended festivals, likely due to the accolades gathered from critics, the reasonable cost of Toronto hotels and the very pleasant autumn weather. Although not as prolific as Cannes, TIFF is quickly gaining in the world stage as the home of many Oscar winners and crowd pleasers, such as *Slumdog Millionaire* and *The King's Speech*.

The Bell Lightbox is a 5-story, horizontal structure with a 42-story residential building at the rear. The contemporary building encompasses both light and shadow and boxes within boxes. The architects at KPMG wanted to create a building full of energy and imagination, and this is evident in their cinemas, studios, restaurants, shops and galleries. The endless sheets of glass reflect the ever-changing panorama of historic King Street during the day, while at night its interior lights illuminate the streetscape like a beacon.

At the main entrance, you are greeted by a 3-story atrium and a dominating, sassy, red escalator leading to the upper floors, creating a fluid sequence of movement to the cinemas above. No need to wear a ball gown – the red stairway makes you feel glittery enough. With your popcorn and soda, you'll beam like a celebrity.

Address 350 King Street West, Toronto, ON M5V 3X5, +1 (416)599-8433, www.tiff.net, customerrelations@tiff.net | Getting there Subway to St. Andrews (Line 1); 504 King streetcar to John Street | Hours Daily 10am–10pm | Tip The TIFF Shop inside the TIFF Bell Lightbox is fabulous, offering a wonderful selection of gifts and books (350 King Street West, Toronto, ON M5V 3X5, www.shop.tiff.net).

99 ___ Tom Thomson's Shack

Vibrant paintings emerge from weather-beaten shack

Tom Thomson was an extraordinary Canadian painter of the early 20th century. He directly influenced Canada's famous art movement as expressed by the Group of Seven. His love of the great outdoors and his ability to translate that passion onto canvas with paints was both his inspiring magic and the roots of his untimely demise.

As an avid fisherman and expert canoeist, he would venture out into the wilderness of Algonquin Park and produce oil sketches of landscapes on small rectangular panels. But it was upon his return to his Toronto shack where he reproduced his gathered scenes onto large canvases, capturing the moody beauty of the ever-changing seasons in nature. Now, they hang as centrepieces in the National Gallery of Canada.

His fellow artist friends banded together and built a cabin in Rosedale Valley in 1915 for Tom Thomson. Partially from economic necessity, and partially from a desire to recreate life in the woods, the shack became cottage, art studio and meeting place for many emerging Canadian painters. He requested a large window to light up the studio and was charged a dollar a month for rent.

On one fateful journey back up to Ontario's north in 1917, Tom Thomson's canoe was found floating close to the dock from where he launched from. His body was discovered eight days later. The enigmatic circumstances of his suspicious death on Canoe Lake has inspired many conspiracy theories and has remained an unsolved mystery for over 100 years.

In homage to Thomson's genius, the shack where he created his most famous masterpiece, *The Jack Pine*, has been moved to the grounds of the McMichael Collection in Kleinburg. Just inside the cabin rests the artist's easel where a version of this famous painting sits. Today, the cabin serves as a shrine commemorating Thomson's woodsman style of living and stupendous works of art.

Tom Thoms
Shack

Cabane de
Thomas

Address 10365 Islington Avenue, Kleinburg, ON L0J 1C0, +1 (905)893-1121, www.mcmichael.com | **Getting there** From downtown Toronto, get on the Gardiner Expressway west, continue to merge to take Ontario-427 north to Highway 27 in Etobicoke. Take the exit toward Eglinton Avenue/Highway 27 from ON-427 north. Get on ON-409 west and take ON 427 north to York Regional Road 99 in Vaughan. Take Highway 27/York Regional Road 27 to the McMichael Gallery. | **Hours** Tue–Sun 10am–4pm | **Tip** Just outside the grounds of the McMichael Canadian Art Collection, explore the hiking trails in the valley behind that display the beauty of Ontario's nature (10365 Islington Avenue, Kleinburg, ON L0J 1C0, www.mcmichael.com).

100 Toronto Music Garden

It is sure to hit the right chord

One wonders if Bach would rejoice if he knew that his *Suite Number 1 in G minor for unaccompanied cello* had been interpreted into a glorious waterfront music garden. Bach is known for his ability to move audiences by the sheer beauty of his music and now this urban delight takes his genius to a different art form. This extraordinarily designed garden with winding treble clef paths and picturesque garden beds is the creation of world-renowned cellist Yo Yo Ma and the creative landscape designer Julie Moir Messervy.

Each of the six sections of this garden gem creatively corresponds to one of the movements of Bach's piece. You begin your garden gait with the well-manicured prelude portrayed by a curve of a riverscape. An alley of Hackberry trees represents measures of music. The Allemande, an age-old German dance, is depicted through a small forest with meandering trails. The Italian/French Courante takes you through a world of wildflowers. The Sarabande, an ancient Spanish dance, is a quiet corner with beautiful stone enclaves for poets and readers alike.

Nearby, minuets comes alive with an arched amphitheater with a stone stage set under a weeping willow tree. In the summer, the garden becomes a concert hall with free classical concerts, inviting both regular fans and out-of-towners. You end the tour at Gigue, a jaunty English dance, on the grassy steps with spectacular views of the harbor.

As we are continually forced to find harmony between a bustling urban life and the need to find inner peace, the quietude of this waterfront wonder becomes essential. One feels the city tension dissolve around you. The opportunity to contemplate waits. No need to be a classical music aficionado. The park is accessible to all and beautiful anytime of the year, so you are sure to be lulled by this garden oasis conveying the works of Johann Sebastian.

Address 479 Queens Quay West, Toronto, ON M5V 3M8, +1 (416)338-0388, www.harbourfrontcentre.com/venues/torontomusicgarden | Getting there Subway to Union (Line 1), take the 509 Harbourfront streetcar to Queens Quay West at Lower Spadina Avenue | Hours Unrestricted | Tip For a great cup of coffee or a cool drink, visit the Music Garden Café adjacent to the garden (466 Queens Quay West, Toronto, ON M5V 2Y3, www.facebook.com/MusicGardenCafe).

101_ Toronto Necropolis

Black history wrapped in Gothic charm

At the edge of the Victorian-era neighbourhood of Cabbagetown, you will find the best example of Gothic Revival architecture in Canada, a place dripping with Gothic charm and the macabre. Walking through the heritage protected neighbourhood, you already feel transported back a hundred years or more. It is fitting that one would find a place for the dead at the end of these streets that would excite the likes of Tim Burton and the urban explorer – the Toronto Necropolis and Cemetery.

A whole *111 Places* book could be written about how the history of the city can be found in this place, featuring gravestones from the first mayor of Toronto, William Lyon Mackenzie, to Joseph Bloore, the founder of the Village of Yorkville. At the corner of the cemetery, the strange story of the re-interment of the early settlers from Potter's Field unfolds, as bodies were moved to the newly opened necropolis in the 1850s. The local government of the day supported new urban development and wanted to move more than 6,000 corpses, but they couldn't find all the bodies or next of kin that would support the move. Only a couple of hundred bodies were actually reburied to the corner of the new necropolis. There is a plaque commemorating the early settlers at the edge of the cemetery between rocky mounds.

Others buried at the necropolis include illuminating civil rights activists who belonged to the black history of Toronto. The Blackburns, a married couple who had a harrowing escape from slavery via the Detroit River into Canada in 1833, built the city's first taxi company and helped build the Little Church at Trinity. The owners of City Cab Company that shuttled around Torontonians helped other black slaves escape the United States and settle in the free city of Toronto. The TTC honours them to this day, using the colour scheme of their company cars on all Toronto public transit.

Address 200 Winchester Street, Toronto, ON M4X 1B7, +1 (416)923-7911, www.mountpleasantgroup.com/Locations/Cemeteries/toronto-necropolis.aspx | **Getting there** Subway to Castle Frank (Line 2), then take 65 Parliament bus to Winchester Street; subway to Broadview (Line 2), then take the 505 Dundas streetcar to Broadview Avenue at Langley Street | **Hours** Daylight Saving Time – Sept 30 8am – 8pm, Oct 1 – Eastern Standard Time 8am – 6pm, Eastern Standard Time–Feb 28 8am – 5:30pm | **Tip** Cross the street and visit the Riverdale Farm, a 3.4-hectare farm that used to be the Riverdale Zoo. Open year round, it offers love and life in fuzzy and feathery forms (201 Winchester Street, Toronto, ON M4X 1B8, www.toronto.ca/explore-enjoy/parks-gardens-beaches/zoos-farms/riverdalefarm).

102 Toronto Popcorn Company

Your movie experience will never be the same

The magical allure of popcorn, the granddaddy of snack food whether enjoyed while watching a movie or discovering a city, is undisputed. So it is appropriate to include a trip to the Toronto Popcorn Company to discover and sample their 100 elaborate flavours of the sumptuous fluffy stuff. We have come a long way since the Iroquois taught Canadian settlers to plant and pop kernels of corn. Today, two recent immigrants from the Philippines have redefined Toronto's gourmet popcorn scene. Customers from far and wide flock to this one-off store in Toronto's Kensington Market.

Joseph and Caramhel Villegas founded the business that evolved from their successful participation in grassroots farmers' markets and pop-ups to its present-day upscale retail store. Toronto Popcorn celebrates not only Toronto but Canada with their patriotic flavours such as Maple Bacon, which combines Canada's love of maple syrup with Hogtown's own passion for bacon. Their best-selling flavour, Sea Salt Maple, is a salute to the sensational mixers in the popcorn crowd. The Popcorn Company relies heavily on local sourcing and their non-GMO corn is locally grown and roasted. Their high-quality product is now often the go-to popcorn for the world-famous Toronto International Film Festival and is easily available at other high-end food purveyors including Saks Fifth Avenue, McEwen's and Fresh and Wild.

Bellying up to their sample bar, you realize that nothing is too strange or exotic to serve as a popcorn flavouring. You consider championing yourself as either a savory or sweet, traditionalist or exotic popcorn aficionado. The choices are endless, and the names are often as elaborate as the flavours, such as the Black Moomba, a Halloween favourite smothered with Belgian white chocolate and coconut. This modern, affordable indulgence is sure to revitalize any movie experience.

Address 147 Baldwin Street, Toronto, ON M5T 3K7, +1 (844)767-8368, www.torontopopcorncompany.com, info@torontopopcorncompany.com | Getting there 505 Dundas streetcar west to Spadina Avenue; 310 Spadina streetcar to Nassau Street | Hours Daily 11am – 8pm | Tip Walk around the corner from the shop to busy Spadina Road, the main artery of Chinatown. A tried and true mainstay for excellent Chinese food is the appropriately named Taste of China. Do order the deep-fried tofu balls with chilli seeds (338 Spadina Avenue, Toronto, ON M5T 2G2, www.tasteofchinarestaurant.ca).

103 __ Toronto's PATH

Fancy getting lost underground?

Perhaps now is the time to explore the 27-kilometre underground retail trail in downtown Toronto. Toronto's PATH is a network of underground pedestrian tunnels and elevated walkways connecting the canyons of office towers in the financial and business district. What started by accident in 1900 to link Toronto's quintessential department store Eaton's to the downtown City Hall has grown like a wildly wandering urban ivy. Even when you don't know where you are, there you are. The PATH offers lots of routes and retail from which to choose.

According to the *Guinness Book of World Records*, the PATH is the largest underground shopping complex in the world. This massive labyrinth connects over 1,200 shops and services. It encompasses more than 50 buildings, five subway entrances, six major hotels and the Union Station railway terminal. People pride themselves on living for much of the year in the PATH and its buildings while protecting themselves from Toronto's severe seasonal extremes. For those looking to be entertained, the PATH connects to Ripley's Aquarium, the CN Tower and the Air Canada Centre. The hallways also link to small historical gems such as the Art Deco ceiling at the CIBC headquarters.

Hop on the PATH and join the 200,000 daily commuters, residents and wandering tourists. At times it will feel like you're swimming upstream as you challenge the masses who are heading towards the subway. You wonder what Jane Jacobs, Toronto's urban planning expert, would think of this departure from street-level stores. With her wisdom that a healthy city's neighbourhoods are reliant on street-level retail versus malls, you wonder if the PATH might be acceptable to Ms. Jacob. Regardless of Toronto's atmospheric conditions, come experience fabulous retail, restaurants and entertainment while swimming among the workaday world of Toronto.

Address See website for map, torontopath.com | **Getting there** Numerous entrances – see website for map | **Hours** See website for individual store hours | **Tip** No trip to Toronto would be complete without a visit to Canada's famous Hockey Hall of Fame. Well labelled on the PATH, the Hockey Hall of Fame celebrates Canada's favourite pastime. Make sure to have a peak at the Stanley Cup, the prized victory trophy (Brookfield Place, 30 Yonge Street, Toronto, ON M5E 1X8, www.hhof.com).

104 Trenton Terrace

A magical real estate solution

If you were teleported back in time to early 1900s Toronto, before the construction of the Gardiner Expressway in the 1950s, the most desirable neighbourhood in Toronto was Parkdale. Its close proximity to Lake Ontario and summer amusements made it one of the most expensive neighbourhoods in the city. Although it has had a difficult period, today this multicultural neighbourhood is very attractive with its wide pedestrian-friendly streets and affordable Victorian homes.

Nestled just off of Calvin Avenue, in the heart of Parkdale, is Trenton Terrace, a hidden laneway. Originally, Trenton Terrace was a single lot property, which was creatively built into nine, south-facing cottages. The businessman John Coatesworth originally built the homes in 1883 as worker tenements. The small, less than desirable dwellings caused great controversy. Public records indicate that local residents representing the upper class attempted to stop these and similar developments in the upscale Parkdale neighbourhood.

Walking down this quaint, car-free laneway, you are transported out of the city to a European neighbourhood or mew corridor of London's Notting Hill Gate. Each residence has its own character and own carefully tended garden. The city surprisingly owns the property rights right up to the front door. With beautiful front decks you ponder if the city pays for their upkeep. Many of the homes have been renovated to be open concept designs with hardwood floors and exposed brick. At a fraction of the price of most Toronto homes, you wonder if we will see more Trenton Terrace-like developments emerging. With the prohibitive real estate prices and growing trend of repurposing of space in today's over crowded cities, it seems like a magical solution. This beautiful terrace, close to great bars, restaurants, indie boutiques and galleries, is a salute to creative urban design.

Address Trenton Terrace, Toronto, ON M6K 1C6 | Getting there 514 Cherry streetcar to Dufferin Street at Springhurst Avenue; 504 King streetcar to Spencer Avenue | Hours Unrestricted | Tip Stop by Palais Royale, a 100-year-old dance hall located at the foot of Roncesvalles Avenue on Lake Ontario. The Palais Royale has been home to great musicians such as Count Basie and Duke Ellington. It is a true period piece and testimony to eras past (1601 Lake Shore Boulevard West, Toronto, ON M6K 3C1, www.palaisroyale.ca).

105 Trinity Bellwoods Gates

Enter into the realm of the white squirrel

At the foot of Queen Street and Strachan Avenue, there's a pair of elegant white arched columns with a wrought-iron gate giving passage to the surreal world of white squirrels frolicking in this downtown park.

Trinity Bellwoods sits on land that's gone through many transformations. It started as a military reserve for the old town of York in the 1700s, and then in 1852 it became Trinity College. The campus was Toronto's first centre of higher learning guided by the prevailing British Anglican ethos. Presently, Trinity College and its representation of academic finery and pomp sits on the grounds of the University of Toronto beside Philosopher's Walk. Only the remnants of the gates remain in their original place as a reminder of what once was there.

The old buildings of Trinity College were demolished in the 1950s, and the gates were left in disrepair until ERA architects, at the request of the city, took on the project in 2004 to reinstate their former glory. Working with an old photograph, they fixed the collapsed archway, and commissioned masonry repairs to reflect the original Victorian beauty of 1904. These white limestone gates hold a clue to the bushy-tailed surprise within.

Pass through these stately gates to enter into the extensive rolling greenery of Trinity Bellwoods Park that serves as an urban playground for young and old alike, with many amenities for outdoor sports and recreation. But what really sets this urban oasis apart is the furry white residents in the trees who frolic and amuse park visitors. Alright Alice, you did not fall down the rabbit hole, and you did indeed see a white squirrel in the park. Urban legend says that they bestow good luck to the fortunate ones who spot the arctic-looking rodent who has its own Twitter account @whitesquirrelTO. Just don't go looking for these elusive creatures during a snow blizzard.

Address 155 Crawford Street, Toronto, ON M6J 2Z0, +1 (416)392-0743, www.trinitybellwoods.ca | Getting there 501 Queen streetcar to Strachan Avenue | Hours Unrestricted | Tip If you didn't see a white squirrel in the park, you can go and console yourself with delicious food and beverages at the White Squirrel Coffee Shop (907 Queen Street West, Toronto, ON M6J 1G5, www.whitesquirrelcoffee.com).

106 Underpass Park

East Enders become the pillars of the commute

Every city seems to have its interpretation of Atlas holding up some celestial orb. Toronto has its own imaginative version, but instead of using Greek gods, Toronto's street artists have used portraits of tough East Enders. These paintings of everyday people hold up the pillars of Toronto's highway overpasses located in the downtown east end.

After much debate about what to do with this completely neglected and derelict space; whether to extend the Gardiner Expressway, tear it down, or create some commercial development, Toronto fortunately decided to create a much-needed recreational space. As part of revitalizing Toronto's waterfront district, all three levels of government helped fund Underpass Park in 2012. The park features a playground, hearty greenery, basketball courts, a skateboard park and 40 huge pillars of street art.

An innovative approach to address the inherent oppressive darkness of the concrete underpasses was the installation of *Mirage* by Paul Raff Studio. This mirrored artwork hangs on the ceiling like a large reflective honeycomb and highlights the interplay of natural light and urban night lights. Underpass Park's urban gallery has been further adorned with cheerful colourful artwork celebrating the work of graffiti and mural creators.

Troy Lovegates and friend Labrona painted 16 portraits of 16 people on 16 pillars. Lovegates explored the east end of Toronto and took photos of residents who captured his imagination and represented a wide range of ages, ethnic backgrounds and occupations. Troy told a local newspaper the pillar portrait characters are 'the pillars of this bridge… the pillars of community holding up the crazy Toronto commute.'

Come walk around Underpass Park and feel a sense of whimsy and community, a stark contrast to the whizzing of traffic overhead. Modern Atlases show up in the most unexpected places.

Address 168 Eastern Avenue, Toronto, ON M4L 3T0, +1 (416)214-1344, www.urbantoronto.ca/database/projects/underpass-park | Getting there 504 King streetcar to River Street, then walk south to the park under the Gardiner Expressway. | Hours Unrestricted | Tip Toronto's newest park, Corktown Common, is a new jewel in the landscape of the West Don Lands. Corktown Common is 7.3 hectares/18 acres at the foot of Lower River Street and Bayview Avenue (www.urbantoronto.ca/database/projects/corktown-common).

107__The Vessel
A buried creek streams through it

This elegant ethereal water sculpture poised within Taddle Creek Park brings a buried stream and its past to the surface. Vessels have appeared throughout the story of our civilization, often being compared to a woman's body. Vessels nurture, contain, and carry; they are curvaceous, often ornate, with a spouted opening. Ilan Sandler's *Vessel* is no exception.

Sandler is an artist who wished to express how the flow of water nourished people throughout history, both practically and spiritually. So when the City of Toronto commissioned him to create a sculpture for Taddle Creek Park, water naturally was to be the main focus. The sculpture turned into a water fountain with unique features that honoured both the past and the future. Standing 5.7 metres, or 19 feet tall, with light pouring through its stainless-steel rods, the silver *Vessel* shimmers behind a veil of water that runs over its rim. It is an avant-garde objet d'art of this century, with its steel and precision welding. For centuries, Taddle Creek ran through downtown Toronto before it got buried underground by development. After almost 200 years, it has come to life again, flowing over the *Vessel*. The steel rods in total measure out 4 kilometres, or 2.5 miles, the approximate length of the creek between the park and Lake Ontario. Therein lies the poetry within Sandler's design.

Water arteries have spurred development in all the major cities of the world, and Toronto is no exception. The Don and Humber rivers frame our downtown core, with Lake Ontario at the base. The Anishinaabe Nation, an Ojibway-speaking people who lived in this area, drew inspiration for their spiritual creation myths from water. And as with the *Vessel*, the earth and waters call forth the elements of a woman. As the Anishinaabe believe, 'the rivers that run underground are the veins of Mother Earth, and water is her blood.'

Address Located at the southwest corner of Lowther Avenue and Bedford Road, in the Annex area of Toronto, www.taddlecreekmag.com/peeling-back-the-layers | **Getting there** Subway to St. George (Line 1 & 2) | **Hours** Unrestricted | **Tip** Walk through the Victorian gates off Bloor Street West just west of the Royal Ontario Museum. Step onto the path of Philosopher's Walk and follow the buried Taddle Creek. It will take you down through the pastoral grounds of the Royal Conservatory of Music and University of Toronto (www.torontoist.com/2016/06/philosophers-walk).

108_ Vog Vault
at Fluevog Shoes

Topsy-turvy space for head-over-heels antics

Canadian shoe designer John Fluevog is famous for his flamboyant, rainbow-hued footwear. Madonna, Alice Cooper, Beyonce and Lady Gaga have all worn them. With their sculptural heels and messages inscribed into the soles, such as his 'Angel' boot engraving, 'resists alkali, water, acid, fatigue and Satan,' his shoe creations are the stuff of pure imagination. A sense of humour mixed with an element of activism.

When John moved his store into a former Queen Street West bank building he designed every room, including the front and back showroom, into a forest-themed wonderland. But what to do with the bank's former vault? In a stroke of perfect marketing genius, Fluevog transformed the back vault into the world's first gravity-defying chamber. Welcome to the Vog Vault! In this magical realm, shoes are not so much about grounding but designed for walking on air. The interior of Vog Vault's illusory space mimics a vintage photo of John and his wife that hangs in all Fluevog shops. Replete with a Victorian love seat and bookshelves, this nine-square-foot room inspires visitors to perform aerial shenanigans and document their acrobatic buoyancy. It is ultimately a place of spontaneous theatre and gleeful drama. Let your imagination soar and turn your world upside down in the most playful manner. Climb walls and ceilings showing off your spidery prowess. Give a solo performance or pose with your fellow circus chums. If your creative juices need a boost, check out the hilarious photos that other Vog Vaulters have posted on Instagram.

Offering ethereal optical illusions, exotic shoes and an exterior wall mural painted by a native Toronto graffiti artist birdO, Fluevog's shoe store and Vog Vault will delight your visual senses. And if laughter heals all, the Vog Vault will transform daily stress and worry into inevitable carnivalesque mirth.

Address 686 Queen Street West, Toronto, ON M6J 1E7, +1 (416)581-1420, www.fluevog.com/stores, toronto@fluevog.com | **Getting there** 501 Queen streetcar to Euclid Avenue, or 7 Bathurst Street bus down to Queen Street West and walk to Euclid Avenue | **Hours** Mon–Wed 11am–7pm, Thu–Sat 10am–8pm, Sun 11am–6pm | **Tip** Now that you have the shoes, it's time to buy unique wardrobe items at Gaspard Shop down the street with its saluation, 'Welcome to our random assembly of beautiful things' (886 Queen Street West, Toronto, ON M6J 1G3, www.gaspardshop.com).

109__The William Meany Maze

Weaving intrigue into gardens

Toronto has also upheld an ancient global tradition. Like the ancient Greeks, Vikings, and Versailles, we also have our own labyrinth. It's the William Meany Maze on Centre Island. It now stands as a place of mysteries and knights in shining armour. In 1967, during the centennial celebrations, and the creation of the Centennial Gardens, The Dutch Association of Canada commissioned a hedge maze. For years, it was a staple on the itinerary as to what there was to do on Toronto Island as a young child.

William Meany, like so many others from Toronto, was no meany at all. He, too, had remembered it to be a 'go to' feature of his childhood in the city. A successful businessman, he wanted to show his colleagues his favourite haunts, only to discover that it had shut down due to disrepair. With nostalgic affection, he had a vision to change that. In 2015, with his donation of $200,000, the maze's revival was underway. Twelve hundred cedars were planted, and cedar chip paths were created, all holding true to the original design of Peter Vanderwerf, the landscape designer in 1967. A new sign that reads 'William Meany Maze' was also erected.

A maze is a predecessor to the adrenaline of the escape room for the mystery lover, a secret garden to hide a hidden kiss from a lover, and a meditation for dreamers in which to get lost. Hedge gardens have a special place in the work of intriguing botany and garden design. Weaving mystery into garden design has been a playful way to explore for Nordic warriors, Sun Kings and modern urban dwellers wanting a challenge.

But most of all, hedge gardens, such as the one found just beside the Centennial Gardens of Centre Island, are places where small feet can run freely with youthful glee, as children rush to explore and compete with themselves and others to find the center of the maze.

Address Avenue of the Island, Toronto, ON | **Getting there** Ferry from Jack Layton Ferry Terminal (9 Queens Quay West, Toronto, ON M5J 2H3, www.toronto.ca/explore-enjoy/parks-gardens-beaches/toronto-island-park/all-ferry-schedules) | **Hours** Daily 8am–11pm | **Tip** Rest your weary feet and escape the shrieks of children at St. Andrew by-the-Lake Anglican Church. This tiny picturesque island chapel is truly worth a visit (Cibola Avenue, Toronto, ON, www.standrewbythelake.com).

110__Wychwood Barns Market
The intersection of community and food

During the 1920s, the Wychwood Barns was the most important transit facility in the city. The complex of five streetcar sheds was a housing and repair facility for the Toronto Civic Railway. Providing a connection within the developing city, these five privately run railways were essential transportation pathways. However, as the role of streetcars in the city diminished, the Barns were decommissioned and set to be demolished. On the eve of the shed's pending destruction, the close-knit Wychwood community came together and repurposed the faltering facility through what would become one of the most transparent and collaborative community efforts in Toronto's history. The Barns now function as a successful community centre and multi-use park, housing an eclectic mix of artistic spaces, non-profits, planting areas and art and farmers' markets.

Walking into the Stop Farmer's Market on a busy Saturday, you are unsure where to begin. Do not be overwhelmed by the enormity of the place, but rather relax into the experience. Consider it a shopping adventure as opposed to a shopping errand. There is a smorgasbord of local farmers' harvests. Just-picked produce, sweet-smelling baked goods, organic meats, raw-milk cheeses and mouth-watering jams populate every table. Open year round, with twice the number of vendors in the summer, the choices are plentiful. Your stomach will begin to speak to you and your olfactory senses will be on overdrive as you smell and sample.

Community looms large in the heritage Barns. Vendors are quick to explain how the Wychwood Market is different than other city markets. You can feel it. Vendors joke and barter with each other while greeting regulars who purchase their weekly staples. You reflect on Jane Jacobs, urban theorist, who would be proud of this well-designed village hub, celebrating both the creativity and capacity of neighbourhoods.

Address 601 Christie Street, Toronto, ON M6G 4C7, +1 (416)597-0335, www.artscapewychwoodbarns.ca | **Getting there** Light Rail St. Clair Avenue West towards Keele to Wychwood Avenue | **Hours** Sat 8am–12:30pm (1pm in the summer); visit the website for weekly special arts and cultural events and exhibitions | **Tip** Join in on the spirit of community and follow a Jane's Walk. Jane Jacob, the urban activist, considered Toronto her home and her legacy is still alive with community-led walking tours celebrating Toronto's neighbourhoods (www.janeswalk.org).

111 The Yorkville Rock

Yorkville Park's chunk of Precambrian Shield

This jutting 600-tonne hunk of Precambrian Shield is one of most grounded meeting spots in the centre of the city. In a move that would make Canadian songwriter Joni Mitchell proud, they took a parking lot, and redesigned an urban park on it after local residents lobbied for three decades for its creation. This stone outcrop is at the side of a block-long, award-winning park that celebrates the diversity of the Canadian landscape and runs along the busy streetscape of the Yorkville area.

'The Rock', as it is known by locals, was harvested from a farm in Gravenhurst, Ontario and brought to Toronto with 20 flatbed trailers. This glacial shield was assembled as an enormous 3D tectonic puzzle, so as to minimize, though not eliminate, the visible joints. It sits atop structural beams that span the roof of the Line 2 subway below.

The Rock is one of several landscape features of the park which include a rain/icicle wall, a marsh, an upland forest and prairie meadows. It was important to represent the Canadian Shield in the design of the park since its horseshoe imprint covers almost half of the country. The Rock is cut out of a billion-year-old eroded mountain range, one of the oldest on our planet. It serves as a counterpoint to all that is new and flashy in Toronto's interpretation of Rodeo Drive.

By its barren simplicity, The Rock invites you to sit with your friend to people watch. The Rock entices children to climb and play and provides seating for outdoor concerts. Some say it's one of the more romantic places in the city, and walking by it on a sultry night certainly confirms this idea. It offers an unmoving, solid, prominent place to meet a friend as they exit the subway right next to it, or a cool respite between the busy neighbouring shops and streams of people. It's easy to say "Hey, let's meet at The Rock" because you're bound to have an adventure.

Address 130 Cumberland Street, Toronto, ON M5R 1A6 | Getting there Subway to Bay (Line 2) | Hours Unrestricted | Tip Just north of The Rock, there are a myriad of high-end art galleries on Hazelton Avenue. To explore Canadian artists that fetch top dollar, visit the Mira Godard Gallery (22 Hazelton Avenue, Toronto, ON M5R 2E2, www.godardgallery.com).

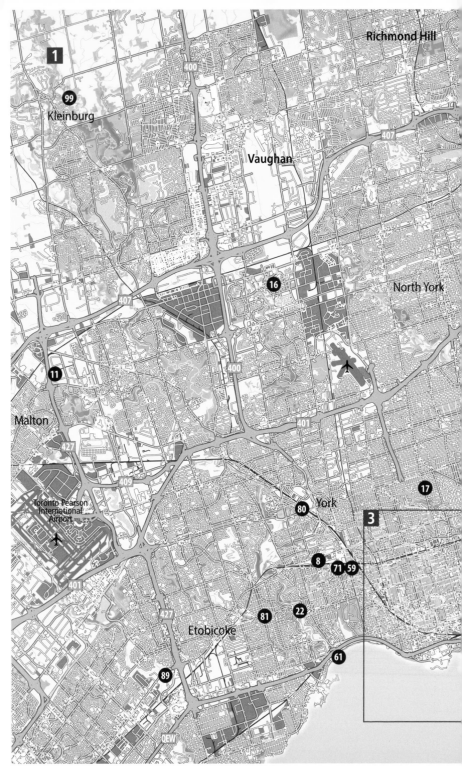

Christoph Hein, Sabine Hein-Seppler
**111 Places in Singapore That You
Shouldn't Miss**
ISBN 978-3-7408-0382-7

John Major, Ed Lefkowicz
**111 Places in Brooklyn
That You Must Not Miss**
ISBN 978-3-7408-0380-3

Wendy Lubovich, Ed Lefkowicz
**111 Museums in New York
That You Must Not Miss**
ISBN 978-3-7408-0379-7

Alexia Amvrazi, Diana Farr Louis,
Diane Shugart
**111 Places in Athens
That You Shouldn't Miss**
ISBN 978-3-7408-0377-3

Benjamin Haas, Leonie Friedrich
**111 Places in Buenos Aires That
You Must Not miss**
ISBN 978-3-7408-0260-8

Beate C. Kirchner
**111 Places in Rio de Janeiro
That You Must Not Miss**
ISBN 978-3-7408-0262-2

Photo Credits

Aga Khan Park (ch. 2): ©Aga Khan Museum; Bad Axe Throwing (ch. 8): Bad Axe Throwing Inc.; BAPS Shri Swaminarayan Mandir (ch. 11): BAPS Shri Swaminarayan Mandir, Toronto; Bata Shoe Museum (ch. 13): Corynn Fowler; Choir!Choir!Choir! (ch. 28): Choir! Choir! Choir!; Cinecycle (ch. 30): Andrew Davies; Evergreen Brick Works (ch. 40): Corynn Fowler; Forbes Wild Foods (ch. 42): Dyson Forbes; Gallery Grill (ch. 44): Gallery Grill at Hart House, Toronto University; Hot Docs Ted Rogers Cinema (ch. 58); Mjölk (ch. 71): Corynn Fowler; Native Child and Family Services Long-house (ch. 73): Jesse Colin Jackson / jessecolinjackson.com; Otto's Berlin Diner (ch. 76): Corynn Fowler; South-Western Bathhouse (ch. 89): Elizabeth Lenell Davies; Tom Thomson's Shack (ch. 99): The McMichael Canadian Art Collection; Trinity Bellwoods Gates (ch. 105): Elizabeth Lenell Davies; Underpass Park (ch. 106): Spencer Wynn/spencerwynn.com; The Vessel (ch. 107): Ilan Sandler

Art Credits

Banksy's Guard with Dog (ch. 10): Banksy; The Cameron House Ten Ants (ch. 20): Napoleon Brousseau; The Gardiner Museum (ch. 45): Greg Payce; Gladstone Hotel (ch. 48): Bruno Billio; Inukshuk Park (ch. 63): Kellypalik Qimirpik; Ireland Park (ch. 64): Rowan Gillespie; The Pasture (ch. 76): Joseph Fafard; Underpass Park (ch. 106): Felix Berube; The Vessel (ch. 107): Ilan Sandler

Anita Mai Genua is a writer, educator and urban explorer. She is a native Torontonian and has worked at Canada's CBC Radio's National News as an editor. She has taught high school, designed software for education and recently, has co-written a book, *Happier With Habits*. As a world traveller, wanderlust and storytelling have always appealed to her. Even in her youth, Anita enjoyed telling stories of her home when she helped co-ordinate an exhibit, 'Life in Canada' under the watchful eye of the KGB in glasnost-era Soviet Estonia. She now lives in downtown Toronto with her husband, two children and dog.

Clare Davenport's insatiable curiousity serves as her beacon for her life's pursuits and professional choices. She has had a varied career as an analyst at Goldman Sachs, an international strategy consultant to the CEO of numerous enterprises including, as of late, a national children's cancer charity. As a certified nutritionist, yoga instructor, and co-author of the book, *Happier with Habits*, she guides others through workshops and blogs. Nothing delights Clare more than helping others travel down their chosen path. She is grateful for the amazing neighbourhoods of Toronto, which have been her home for the last 20 years. Clare can often be found exploring and photographing the city with her husband, four children and two dogs.

Elizabeth Lenell Davies mixes architecture and design with intentional acts of urban acupuncture to positively transform communities. After completing her Masters in Architecture in Los Angeles, she worked on the design of the Bangkok Contemporary Art Museum. The architectural model, made to fit in a travelling suitcase, connected LA, Bangkok and New York. While in New York, she co-wrote *The (Cosmos)etic Case*, a pithy book distributed by Printed Matter. Elizabeth currently resides with her family in Toronto, where she teaches an architectural program for the arts organization No.9, called 'Imagining My Sustainable City,' to thousands of youth in diverse neighbourhoods. She is passionate about inspiring the next generation to envision building a sustainable Toronto.

Acknowledgement

The richness of this book is due to the coming together of the three unique perspectives of Anita, Clare and Elizabeth, who collaborated in celebrating the great city of Toronto. We thank the fabulous Torontonians – the artists, entrepreneurs, curators and engaged residents – whom we have met along this journey.

Anita would like to thank Christina Prozes and Heily Teasdale for their ideas and direction. An even bigger thank you goes out to the amazing Annalisa Luik, who consistently held her hand and words with conviction. Finally, a big kiss to her husband Tony who has embraced exploring the 6ix with her on his side for decades.

Clare would like to thank her wonderful husband John who patiently explored and photographed the city with her on early weekend mornings. She would also like to thank her children Tucker, Tate, Liam and Sidney for paddling down rivers, exploring Toronto beaches, sampling foreign foods and discovering hidden hideaways. Finally, Clare would like to thank her magnificent mother Sheila who edited submissions and visited magical gardens and teashops. It has been a gift to her to have her family by her side.

Elizabeth would like to thank all of the members of her creative crowd, notably Andrew Davies, who have contributed their ideas and given her encouragement.

We would also like to thank Karen Seiger and Laura Olk for their hard work and support in bringing this project to fruition.